# Slices of Life

# Slices of Life

Altha F. Manning

Copyright © 2012 by Altha F. Manning.

Library of Congress Control Number:    2011961477
ISBN:          Hardcover              978-1-4691-4645-4
               Softcover              978-1-4691-4644-7
               Ebook                  978-1-4691-4646-1

All rights reserved. No part of this book may be reproduced or transmitted in any form or by any means, electronic or mechanical, including photocopying, recording, or by any information storage and retrieval system, without permission in writing from the copyright owner.

This book was printed in the United States of America.

**To order additional copies of this book, contact:**
Xlibris Corporation
1-888-795-4274
www.Xlibris.com
Orders@Xlibris.com
107485

# Contents

Dedication ..................................................................................ix
Acknowledgments.....................................................................xi
Introduction ................................................................................1

## Daily Living

What Is Living? ............................................................................5
Everything Changes ...................................................................7
On Being Me, on Being You: A Chosen Reality .......................8
Antithesis .....................................................................................9
I Treasure You ...........................................................................10
Don't Try ....................................................................................11
Hopeful Wishes .........................................................................12
Humor: The Sunshine of Life...................................................13
I Understand . . . I Don't Understand .....................................14
I'm Lost ......................................................................................15
Illusion .......................................................................................16
In Affairs of Nature ...................................................................17
Janine, Living Death ................................................................18
A Child Is Born: A Letter to Earnest Elijah ............................20
My Mind.....................................................................................21
Naturals .....................................................................................22
No Time......................................................................................23
On Life and Death—A Request of a Friend ..........................24
Gone Far Too Soon ..................................................................27
Happy Valentine's! ...................................................................30
One Never Knows ....................................................................31
Silent Voice ...............................................................................32
Another Chance at Life ...........................................................33

You Jus Hav to be Der ..................................................................... 38
The Wind I ........................................................................................ 39
The Wind II ....................................................................................... 40

## Celebrating Family

A Beautiful Day to Remember ....................................................... 43
A Birthday Wish for Aunt Eleanor .................................................. 44
Christmas 2006 ................................................................................. 45
Happy Birthday, Russell! ................................................................. 47
Happy Thanksgiving ....................................................................... 50
Russell's Dad's Birthday ................................................................. 51
Russell's Valentine . . . 2003 ........................................................... 53
Christmas 2004 and Before for the Flowers Family ..................... 54
Lessons Learned .............................................................................. 67

## Love

What Is Love? .................................................................................. 77
Love Is a Many-Splendored Thing ................................................ 78
An Ode to You ................................................................................. 79
Distractions ...................................................................................... 80
Do You Feel it? ................................................................................. 81
Fear of Loving .................................................................................. 82
I Did It! .............................................................................................. 83
I Dreamed of You ............................................................................ 84
I Love Your . . ................................................................................... 85
I Miss You ......................................................................................... 86
I Wish You Love ............................................................................... 87
I Wonder .......................................................................................... 88
Impromptu Visit ............................................................................... 89
Love Is Like . . . ................................................................................. 90
Love of a Lifetime ........................................................................... 91

My Loss, My World ............................................................................. 92
You Are Always There, Here in My Heart ........................................ 93
It........ ................................................................................................. 94
The Dilemma of Moonlight Love ..................................................... 95
Priorities............................................................................................... 96
The Lonely Trek .................................................................................. 97
The Question Is................................................................................... 98
Transformation ................................................................................. 100

## Friendship

Merry Christmas 2007 ..................................................................... 103
Happy Father's Day ........................................................................ 105
Happy New Year!............................................................................. 106
Missing My Friend ............................................................................ 107
My Friend, the Great Leader ......................................................... 108
Semba ............................................................................................... 110
A Note from a Friend ...................................................................... 111
My Friends, My Village ................................................................... 112
This Christmas, 2001 ........................................................................ 118
You Were Just Here and *Poof*, You're Gone ............................... 120

## Loss and Grief

Grieving............................................................................................. 125
Holidays—Christmas and New Year's 2003 ................................. 128
A Treasured Jewel........................................................................... 130
A Journey through Loss and Grief ................................................ 131

## Spirituality

Thanksgiving 2001 ........................................................................... 138
Church............................................................................................... 140
Thanksgiving .................................................................................... 142
I Care About . . . ............................................................................. 144

## Travel

Zanzibar ...................................................................................................147
China, Into the Future! ..........................................................................150
Jamaica, No Problem Mon at Dunn's River Falls .........................................155

## Aging

Living Elegantly, Aging Gracefully ...............................................................159

# Dedication

**IN MEMORY OF**

My deceased grand daddy, Herbert G. Hadley; MaDear, Aldonia Hadley Flowers; DaDoby, William Doby Flowers Sr.;

My deceased husband, George, who is the inspiration for most of the book;

My brother Junior; and Cousin Doug.

Thanks for the wonderful Lessons that guide me and the beautiful memories that are carved in my heart.

**AND TO**

Russell, my son, who is the "sunshine" of my life. Thanks for being you and for giving me hope for tomorrow.

# Acknowledgments

I have been helped in the production of this book by my niece Keiba who first read my selections and researched publishers for me. My editor friends Carolyn Holifield and Gail Thompkins and Cousin Debra Austin read it and made suggestions that enabled me to make improvements in the manuscript and format. They along with my friend Betty Anthony, sister Doby Flowers, Cousin Gene Telfair and my son Russell Manning also reviewed each draft and suggested revisions.

My cousin Gene and my "young" friends Byron Greene and Darrell Winfrey assisted me with my technology needs.

For their support and encouragement: My sisters and brothers; nephews and nieces and their children whose lives bring me joy, inspiration and hope for the future; and all of my extended family;

My many friends across the country and beyond and those young folk who have allowed me to be an influence in their lives but who influence me even more;

And to my village caretakers, who supported me in my growing up years and beyond.

I am eternally grateful for their instructions, feedback, continuing support, and encouragement.

Thanks to all.

# Introduction

Producing this book has been a labor of love that was developed over a long period of my life. As long as I can remember, I recorded memorable times, places, events, and people or even the simple daily mundane events of life. My very earliest writings I think were my best because they were raw but were lost in moves and later from two viral computer crashes.

I was a dreamer day and night and had a vivid imagination. I've always used it to escape from whatever I was attempting to avoid or to just fast forward myself to another place of relaxation or whatever my mind was searching for. It was also a convenient tool for problem solving. I even worried at times that I might not come back from some of those imaginary trips.

This book is an attempt to capture both the very special moments of life as well as the ordinary. Life's events, though rhythmic, happen randomly and concurrently. At the exact moment someone is dying another is being born, and others are doing all the things that life presents and allows. I have tried to capture some of those experiences and though they are my own, hopefully, they will resonate with the reader. These reflections are not meant to be representative of all of life's experiences, simply parts, hence, slices of life. It is life as I saw it. Someone looking at the same situation may see it differently; but these pages reflect my interpretation of the various experiences presented here.

My parents had a tremendous influence on me. They saw raising their six children as their mission in life, and they made many sacrifices to do so. As I reviewed the selections, I present in this book, I was amazed at how much of that early training stayed with me. Those experiences helped to shape who I am. Of course, growing up in a household of six children and two adults, meant that there was activity all the time. As the oldest child, I was often charged with caring for the younger ones and carrying out my parents dictates. However, I also saw them as my little precious gems when they were small. They too had a significant influence on me, and it was through them that we bonded as a family. Although there is a section titled "Love," the theme and feelings of love are woven throughout the tapestry of the entire book.

As I ventured out on my own, married, and then had my son, many others became a part of my life. They were friends, mentors, neighbors, professional associates, etc. Friendships, experiences with and through them are captured as well as my love life, spirituality, marriage, and my son's role in our lives. The inevitable death and the resultant sense of loss and grief are captured through my lens. Although I caution that death is not the sole proprietor of loss, it can be one of the most devastating. Loss can come from severing ties with a loved one, the loss of an endeared pet, a friend, or any number of things. No matter what the loss is, grief follows.

Opportunities to see and experience the world beyond the neighborhood were always prominent among my goals. Even as a child, I traveled from home to south Florida to see my grandparents. At times my grandparents as well as other relatives would take me on trips to places like New York, Atlanta, and Chicago. I don't know whether those early trips imprinted the desire to travel and try new things or whether it is just in my genes. No matter, I am an avid fan of travel and new experiences through it. It brings real meaning to broadening one's horizons. It helps one to see that we are truly connected to other people, cultures, and countries and their corresponding political structures as nations and that our interdependence and interrelatedness are not just glib terms thrown around recklessly; they are real. I have traveled fairly extensively both in the United States and internationally. I share here a few of those experiences, and how they influenced me. Although I list Egypt and China among the places I want to go, since that selection was written, I have traveled to both. However, only China is featured among these selections.

Although I am not a humorous person, I often see the humor in real life situations. I also don't tell jokes well, but I love to hear them and other funny stories. I love the resultant laughter that comes from listening to, seeing, or reading them. Most importantly, I realize that humor serves an essential purpose in life. I share my views on humor in one of the selections and also describe the process of aging in a dry humorous fashion. It is a process that will happen to all of us if we continue to live.

# Daily Living

# What Is Living?

Living is anticipating the sunrise and admiring the sunset;

Living is observing a caterpillar transform and a butterfly slowly emerge from its cocoon;

Living is watching dolphins play in the surf;

Living is listening to the soothing, rough sounds of rushing waves;

Living is seeing a budding flower unfold and appreciating its evolution;

Living is observing the bee pollinate flowers and appreciating the sweet taste of its fresh honey;

Living is loving the rain as much as the sunshine and the smell of freshness following a rainfall;

Living is reaching the top of the mountain and staring out at all that nature offers;

Living is listening to a beautiful song, feeling, and swaying to its melody;

Living is watching lovers whisper in each other's ears; touch each other's lips;

Living is bathing in the love of another and giving love unconditionally;

Living is helping the old walk and hold on, listening and reveling in their wisdom;

Living is holding a baby and watching the discovery of everything old as new;

Living is being with a good friend, talking, listening, seeing his silence and loving it, reading his mind, saying his words and feeling comfortable, laughing, trusting and being as one.

Living is enjoying who and where you are.

Living is dreaming of tomorrows and making those dreams come true!

# Everything Changes

Everything changes.
The seed is planted,
grows into a plant,
blossoms and its flower falls to the ground.

The leaf unfurls,
It beams a bright green,
Its colorful glory lights the fall,
And fades into decay.
Day turns to dusk then night
And the sun soon rises.

The child becomes a man,
The man fades away,
Life begins anew with birth.
We praise, we mourn,
We laugh, we cry.

Love awakens.
It blossoms,
It is tested, it wanes,
It survives, it is weakened,
It is strengthened and thrives.
Nothing remains the same.

# On Being Me, on Being You: A Chosen Reality

The truth as I believe it is the reality I have created.
Some of my reality overlaps with your reality, and yours and yours.
Are any two realities ever the same?

My reality changes.
Does it make what it has changed from now wrong?
Is my new reality not ever totally new?
Is it now right?
The frequency of reality shifts;
Blossoming, ballooning, shrinking, tightening, and loosening!

Does it define me? Is it who I am?
Can I step outside my reality;
Inside it; away from it?
Can I lay it bare and examine it?
Do I mold it or does it mold me?

# Antithesis

Fog over an icy lake is but one

A voice and its echoes are but one

Our hearts, our thoughts, our ways descend from one

Life—death

Love—hate

Joy—sorrow

Pain—pleasure

Omnipresent—humiliating—fulfilling

In their oneness

# I Treasure You

I can't imagine life without you.
I want your advice, your friendship.
I trust you with my private thoughts.
Things I'd never consider discussing with others,
I fluidly and without reservation discuss with you.
I seek your advice and counsel.
I treasure your candid and sometimes humorous answers.

Although, I wish you'd slow down, take on less, give less at the "store," and give me more of you,
I admire and deeply respect your
Commitment and dedication,
Your contributions to developing and advancing your cause.
You truly make a difference!

I've learned a lot about living from you and I treasure every lesson.

# Don't Try

We can't describe it,

We can't hide it,

Nor can we deny it,

It's another of nature's miracles.

## Hopeful Wishes

Here's hoping sunshine for your day,

"flowers" to surround you,

beauty in abundance,

white figurines in blue skies,

faith to uphold you, and

love in your heart.

Please know that you are in my heart.

# Humor: The Sunshine of Life

The sun may not shine every day.
Its rays of light may not penetrate your windows.
But we can choose to smile, to see the bright side of the situation, of life.
We can choose to laugh at ourselves; the mismatched black and brown socks,
That the glasses we are looking for are on our eyes, and the missing watch on our arm.

Laughter emanates from the soul and penetrates the heart.
Your face lights up and brightens all around you.
A good healthy dose of laughter everyday helps to adjust our perspective, our outlook on life.
It helps us to see more clearly, to sift through the scraps of life, pick out its valuables, and discard the trash.

A sense of humor and its resultant laughter prepares the mind to deal with life's frailties, our faults, our shortcomings, our failures. It helps us to get up and try again, to turn a situation around, and to see a problem simply as a challenge to meet and an opportunity born. Having a sense of humor, allows us to laugh at ourselves, to let our defenses down so that solutions can enter through the gate.

This great ability above all else generates sunshine in our hearts, lightens our load, and—our souls. It works from the inside out, and the outside in. You can't laugh and be mad at the same time.

# I Understand . . . I Don't Understand

Work is important, I understand
There is not enough time to do the things you must do, I understand
They are important and your priorities, I understand
Rest and play are essential to a balanced life, I understand
Nothing must crowd your space, I understand
There's only time for those for whom you choose
Your priorities are set by you
There is no time, no room, no space for me, . . . I don't understand

# I'm Lost

It seems I've lost my sense of direction.

My compass no longer works.

I know that in time I will survive, and hopefully thrive.

But in this moment, at this time,

I am bombarded with a million thoughts,

images, perceptions, reflections.

They all converge from my brain to my heart

And leave my fragile heart impotent.

I must gather my senses, strengthen my resolve, and

Like the turtle, slowly rebuild my delicate me.

# Illusion

I've looked, and tried to see

I've heard, and tried to listen

Heartbeats, thoughts, fears and joy engulf me

Understanding is illusive

As time races by, but stands still.

# In Affairs of Nature

When pain exceeds pleasure

When sadness conquers joy

Where masks cover the face

And the heart becomes a toy

The time is now and not tomorrow

To end the never ending sorrow

# Janine, Living Death

As she laid there, her body severely withered and immobile, I silently prayed and cried, Lord why? Her head, her hair, her face were the same; healthy looking, even gorgeous. The hands and arms were uncovered, long, and spiny as skin draped over bone. The rest of her could be discerned from the cover. A small, very small frame that couldn't move lay there motionless, except to move her mouth as the suction instrument removed the saliva, and to mimic words with no sound. In fact, the only other part of her that did move was her right arm sliding slowly, slowly from her side to the side of the bed where I stood. She lipped words which I frequently couldn't understand. The letter chart stood on the window sill with a sign from Michelle asking that we use the chart. I think that was what she was trying to get me to do, Russ was the best at understanding her. Though I stood there and said "I love you," I was torn apart inside. I could feel my intestines rippling, my ears straining to hear what she couldn't say, my flesh curdling over itself, and my head spinning. Oh God, Why?

I had come face-to-face with Janine, a cousin, a consort in "crime" during our childhood. Oh, those days flooded my memory. I could see her poised and graceful, reticent to venture into the unknown, being chided by me to take the risks of her life. "Jump, jump, run, run, and here they come. We're 'gonna get caught,'" as we invaded the secret tomb of the funeral home to take a sneak peak at the dead bodies. And the next day, I acted as if nothing had happened while assuring her that I wouldn't tell. She was always so prim and proper in those days, the favored one. I was adventuresome, egging her on. She discovered boys long before me, and swore me to secrets that didn't have to be. I made a habit of not remembering anyway. We'd sit up late nights with Johnyta and make up stuff and share our dreams, dreams that took us far away like thirty miles, or to New York, or to some other places we'd read about. New York was her favorite place, and she ended up going there for college. We read a lot and dreamed a lot.

As the years passed, she had Michelle, the love of her life. Truly her love, it was Michelle who looked after her mother. That day as we were leaving the hospital, I said to my son, Russell, "Unplug me if it gets to that". I had met living death, Janine hooked up to all the machines, unable to control or do anything for herself, but fully aware of all around her. That is the tragedy of ALS, Lou Gehrig's disease—living death.

# A Child Is Born: A Letter to Earnest Elijah

My Dearest Earnest Elijah,

How happy I was to learn of your birth. I celebrated with all who know and love your parents. You are a fortunate child and gorgeous, I might add. You are loved, treasured, and were hoped for as far too many other babies cannot claim.

You are blessed to be born to two parents who love each other and love you beyond measure. Your Aunt Dee is bubbling over with love and pride, and will always be there for you. And I know that your DeLoach grandparents are smiling and rejoicing in heaven. I was lucky enough to know them and to be considered a friend. The last time I saw your Grandma Eunice she wanted to be here to meet you, hold you, and show you all the love that she has for you. Your grandpa would have bounced you on his knee and watched over you as the precious gem that you are.

I know that you are a good boy and that you will enjoy a loving, happy, and fun-filled childhood. May you dream many sweet dreams; paint many pictures for your parents to put on the walls and the refrigerator; write many poems; write your own stories and make your own books; play in the mud and trample through the house (oops!); read as many books as you can; make airplanes, boats, cars, and solve all the puzzles your parents can find for you; make some puzzles of your own, and unravel life's puzzles; love learning and enjoy life!

Earnest Elijah, may you continue to fill life with happiness, joy, and lots of laughter!

With all my love,

"Grand Auntie" Altha

PS. A little something for you to enjoy later is enclosed!

# My Mind

My mind can go places I've never been
See things I've never seen
Do things I've never done
Taste things I've never tasted
Hear things I've never heard
Feel what I've never felt
Sense what I can't see or hear
Experience the ecstasy, the depth of a world unknown.

My mind is a maze of intrigue;
A map to discover the unknown;
A pathway to solutions; the answer to a problem; the unknown infinity.
My mind holds the possibilities, the dreams, and the horizons unlimited.
It knows no boundaries.
It searches the depths of the sea; scouts the billowing sky; scans the land
    from a distance, and
Zeroes in to the tiniest spectacle of life.
My mind is a-maz-ing!

# Naturals

See the sunshine

See the moonlight

See my love

We are not alone.

Steal a rainbow

Catch a star

All of nature

Is as we are.

# No Time

Why, oh why does it have to be?

No time for you and no time for me?

Hours that linger like endless years

A pierced heart, swelling eyes then trickling tears,

Wishes and hopes that fade as the dusk sets

Suppression in the dark to sublet

Fears that will emerge in the morrow

Wanting time as one to beg, steal or borrow.

# On Life and Death—A Request of a Friend

Right now, my shoulder is twitching. I am having muscle spasms. The pain medicine's effects are shorter and my in-between sleep time is also shorter. Nonetheless, I want to communicate with you before I take my regular dose of pain sedatives to explain my request of a dear friend (what may have seemed to you melodramatic or morbid; one that I failed to communicate earlier).

Ya' know, death (George's) has taught me many lessons. I suppose that anyone who loses someone of a like nature has the same lessons and challenges before them to learn, put aside for later or never or to simply ignore. This last in a chain of many caught me by surprise.

When I went for my pre-op appointment and for the MRI, I was asked the usual questions and given the living will and advanced directives that include designating a surrogate as well as others who would follow through with my wishes in case of severe medical outcomes, e.g., if I went into a coma and doctors saw no hope of improvement, etc.

Now you must understand that I have had many surgeries, some serious and some not as. And, through the years I have been fearless. My usual response to anything that was wrong that could be corrected or removed by surgery was to have the surgery. However, never before did I give a second thought to the possibility of death. In fact, I took it all so lightly. C'est la vie—that's life or in my thinking, death is life. Somehow, I was drawn to take the forms and like a magnet, drawn to complete them. My responses have changed from what I argued about philosophically with my sisters and brothers and friends. I chose to disconnect life support, to eliminate artificial means of sustaining life and if given the option would choose death over life if the quality of life is minimal or non-existent. That's a *bigggg* change for me or maybe a lesson learned. In the past, I wanted to stay alive no matter what because who knew if I would overcome whatever the condition. And I always thought that I could overcome anything!

This upcoming surgery brought me face-to-face with my immortality. I never cared before one way or the other. In fact, I think that I thought that I would live forever or that death was not something I really needed to deal with as it related to me. Why that made me sad, was something I had to explore but it was an exploration I was just beginning and needed more time to come to grips with. The impending surgery dictated that I might not have the time and that the possibility of death is real. Never mind that this was not an emergency or even a life threatening surgery. However, that revelation stunned me. If George had been living as he was when I had most other surgeries, I probably wouldn't have given a thought to it because I had confidence that he would deal with whatever needed to be dealt with effectively and fairly. I suppose too, that the prospects became more real in light of his death, the deaths of my brother, cousin and friend.

But what is it about death that scares me and others? Do I think that I will be missing something or that someone will be missing me? Why would that matter? I suppose because I know that the loved ones left behind would have difficulty dealing with my absence and while here I can empathize with their pain and loss. And maybe I think that I will miss out on something . . . being with special people, being there for them, enjoying their company, their love and the gifts of themselves intertwined with me. Not being able to share their future and to help shape it, like with grandchildren, or continuing to guide my son.

Now, that's a topic for another discussion. My guidance is subtle most times and indirect. Hopefully, he has that inner voice that serves as his compass and helps to direct him. But still, there is that tendency to want things to go right and to be nearby, not hovering, when they don't; to help him see the lessons. And to ensure that he has the tenacity, resilience, intestinal fortitude, a deep and abiding sense of responsibility and commitment; a strong moral compass; a willingness to extend a helping hand; that he can stand alone when necessary; and can deal the right hand in ambiguous situations. Even though he's just turned twenty-nine, he still has lessons to learn that he won't master until he has failures and has survived conflicts and challenges that to him at the time will seem insurmountable.

That brings me to my request, I suppose he asked, "Why me?" Well, it is only natural that I want the two of the most important persons in my life to share what there was of me and what remains—memories, lessons, challenges, laughter, fear and conquering it, thoughts and more thoughts. He can help my son and I think my son can help him.

Here's hoping you have a safe and productive trip and that we can continue to have our philosophical discussions. Ya' know something? You're helping me to sort some of these fuzzy issues out. Now I have saved the best for later. I haven't wanted to put our budding friendship to the ultimate test.

As usual, I have taken the long way around to explain a simple phenomenon. Well, it wouldn't be a phenomenon if it were simple. The request is that you connect and engage with my son in the event of my death; sort of look over him and gently guide him by helping to steer him on the "right" path when he seems to be getting off track. Share with him your philosophy. He will be missing that and will enjoy the sharing. I thank you in advance.

# Gone Far Too Soon

He was here for only a little while and in a whirlwind of turbulence he disappeared. We met, he departed, and in between we lived. And how we lived! What happened in between is the story of a true and lifelong love, the real thing, the love that you could take to the bank, the life of a man who loved fearlessly and gave everything asking nothing in return. Because he gave so freely, he got everything, love twofold and the heart of his beloved.

Soul mates! Lovers! Friends! Confidantes! Mirror minds! We were all of these and more. We were each others' sanctuary from the outside world. Once we stepped into our home, we shut the rest of the world out if needed but discussed it and shared it, taking it apart, and putting it back together again as our preferred world. We could sit in silence and enjoy each other's company or hold deep conversations exploring some of the most difficult and personal topics sometimes agreeing and sometimes disagreeing agreeably. We could laugh at ourselves and each other without offending the other. However, we were sensitive to each other's needs and jumped to meet them.

We could be different and accept those differences, neither requiring the other to bend to our preferences. He liked liver and I despised it. I'd get liver for him or he'd go to his favorite "liver" restaurant to get it. I liked 'chitlins and he despised them although he tried them and had begun to tolerate them. He'd buy them for me. He liked jazz and playing it loudly until the house vibrated and early on in our marriage that was my signal to leave the house to him. I liked country but he thought that I was a Neanderthal. In the end, we both began to listen to each other's music and I even liked a few jazz selections. I used to chide him that jazz didn't make any sense but that country always told a story. We both liked R&B and classical music and often shared them together. When we'd take car trips he always drove and would have music we both liked. Later when our son joined us he even played his music. I'd sit in the back and try to tune them out.

Sometimes the differences were more serious. I liked the yard, flowers, trees, and some ornamentation. He cared nothing for the yard. He even suggested when we lived in Daytona that we have the yard filled with rocks and had already contracted to have it done. I hit the ceiling and told him that was a deal breaker. It was obvious that he cared nothing for the "natural" beauty that I appreciated in nature. I was an environmentalist who he called a "tree hugger" and he was a "pragmatist" as he called himself. The trees got in the way and caused all kinds of damage. They interfered with the utility lines and fell on houses and cars and caused untold damage during storms. When Hurricane Kate hit Tallahassee in 1986 that just proved his point. Boy did he use that! But I never gave in and just kept "hugging my trees." To his dismay, our son was also a "tree hugger." In his official capacity, he supported converting a wooded area near our home to a development. The neighborhood kids used it as a free range and park to play in. As the city was preparing to chop down the trees, our son and his buddies were carrying homemade signs to "Save the trees." He was shocked and angry wanting to know. "What the hell is he doing?"

I replied, "What we taught him to do. Stand up for what he believes in." We both sat and talked with him explaining both sides. Our son kept his position intact and realized that it was private property and that the owner had the right to do with it whatever the ordinances would allow. I secretly wished he and his buddies had gone to the city council to stand their ground.

We could not shop without shopping for the other. Never a major holiday or special day would pass without thoughtful and creative giving. He liked humorous and trick gifts and always included at least one along with the ones that showed his love and caring. I liked more serious and traditional gifts and more modern and sometimes fashionable (outlandish to him) styles for him. I'd buy them and give them to him and he would vow to never wear them and he didn't. I also liked the very personal ones like sexy and matching briefs. He'd model them for me but his conservatism wouldn't allow him to wear them often if ever. As I traveled, just like him, I couldn't pass a fine men's store without looking for a gift for him. When I couldn't find anything else, it was a tie that I bought. He had ties to burn. Some he liked and others he didn't and he didn't wear them either. He'd buy special pieces of one of my favorite designers, jewelry, a purse, a scarf, or even a whole outfit. He liked cards and poetry books and was forever selecting just the right one for me; most often, "just because."

He must have spent hours in card shops searching for just the right verse. I'd receive them on special days but often I got them, "just because." I, on the other hand, seldom bought cards but wrote notes to him. When he left me, I found them all secure and packaged as if in a treasure chest. He too would write notes. I still have mine bundled carefully. He, like me, was a very private person. After he teased that he never got "soppy", I'd threaten to publish his early love letters to prove that he once loved me. He'd say, "I never wrote that stuff." Sometimes I'd go and pull an old letter out or a note he'd put in a book at a page he wanted me to read and read it to him. He'd chase me around the house pretending to try and snatch the letter. Then he'd read it and say, "Who in his right mind would write something like this? I can't imagine who that guy is! He must have been under the influence". I would say, "Yes, he was under the Altha influence and couldn't help himself." We'd both laugh and hug.

Come to think of it, we hugged often and kissed every day. It was a vow we made early in our marriage which for most days we kept. There were only a few days that we pouted and didn't. We seldom went to bed angry and most times we made up before going to sleep. And, before he went to sleep for the last time, I hugged and kissed him for all of those last few hours and whispered love notes in his ears. I knew he understood . . . . I miss him still!

# Happy Valentine's!

*I wish for you that*

*your love is appreciated;*

*you are surrounded by loved ones;*

*your wishes come true;*

*you find peace, hope, joy*

*and happiness;*

*your light shines brightly and*

*illuminates the world around you;*

*people recognize, and appreciate you, and the*

*talents that you bring;*

*most of all that you are loved and*

*know that I love you.*

## One Never Knows

You know, one never really knows what life has in store. I have two very special friends and their families and friends who are in deep pain now. One friend passed on Monday but I didn't learn until yesterday. We "knew" she wouldn't see 2004 but didn't know that since 2003 was so very close, that it would only be a distant vapor for her.

There are surprises around every bend and beneath every footstep. My dear friends here are terrorized by a surprising turn of fate. Their loved one and my friend, lies unconscious this very moment in the hospital. He's diabetic and developed an infection on one of his toes. I just saw him on Sunday and was in the room visiting him when he was scheduled for vascular tests on Monday. Well, he had an allergic reaction to the anesthesia and has not been conscious since. I didn't realize that until late last night while having dinner with other friends that he was at risk not only of losing some toes but his life. One friend commented that he was in critical condition in the Vascular ICU. I was shocked. When I last saw him, things were looking up and he and his fiancée were planning for their spring wedding. They were so exuberant and looking forward to a happy future. Then the vapor took it all away.

Hopefully, we can all extract the good that appears to be hidden beneath a blanket of fear and bask in tomorrow's sunshine. I didn't think you would mind me sharing these thoughts with you on this day of hope. Enjoy the day. Walk with me and talk to me. Hold me close in your heart and prayers.

# Silent Voice

Be still silent voice of rage within.
Allow the calm and cool façade to encage you.
A smile, then a laugh emerges as victors on the battlefield.
Tension and tears be still.

Wanting to go and wanting to stay;
To be alone even in a crowd;
Feeling happy yet sad;
Thoughts must not be spoken aloud.

What's this turmoil that lingers,
Like billowing clouds in the sky?
Formations of doom roar and loom,
Infinitely it seems.
Unfolding light and clarity,
Never disclosing the secret.

Be still my heart. Let it rest for now.
Hold on; let the calming enter your soul!

# Another Chance at Life

Have you ever imagined being told that you have a life-threatening condition?

"How are you doing?" he asks as he enters the room.

"You tell me!" I responded.

"Oh, you're fine," he says.

"Well, that's good news!"

Somehow, I knew that was not the end of that conversation or all that would be on the table for the consultation. He went on to explain the esophageal condition and my hiatal hernia. But these things were not that serious. He went to the next group of photos of my colon and began to explain the polyp that he had removed during my colonoscopy. "However, we do have an area of concern here." My heart began to pound as my head predicted what was to follow . . . *chatter, chatter, chatter,* . . . *noise, noise, noise!* Reverberating through my head was the admonition of the last two years in a row that I only needed a colonoscopy every five years and that he would not allow me to have one earlier . . . *chatter* . . .

"I recommend that you have a CAT scan and see a surgeon." This is what has happened, . . . and would likely happen. No matter how hard I tried, I couldn't hold back the tears that slowly drifted down my cheek. I was forced to ask for a tissue. He gently touched my hand to comfort me. I began to ask questions and he provided answers when he could and made recommendations . . . . *Chatter, chatter, chatter* . . . All I could think of was my son and how this would affect him and how I would deliver the news. You see, my deceased husband had colon cancer. Then the doctor said that he would call my primary physician and that they would make arrangements for me to see a surgeon. I asked who he would want to see if he were me. He gave several names and explanations but noted again that my primary physician would have to make the recommendation and that he would call me.

Thus began my encounter with what I thought then was the face of death. I had always wondered how I would take it if told the dreaded news—you have cancer. Well, I was shaken. I decided then that I wouldn't tell anyone until I had mapped out the landscape and knew with certainty what was to happen. This plan would delay the dreaded outpouring of sympathy . . . and pity. I didn't want to endure that. I thought about my son and my mom who was recovering from a major illness, how my youngest sister would take it, my brothers, my other sister, nieces, nephews, and grandnieces, and nephews.

I left the office and went back to work. I decided not to go home and cry. Though a bit unsettling, work again came through and diverted my attention some, though not all the way. It was just my luck that the landscaper called to say that he would meet me at the house to correct the sprinkler system at around 2:00 p.m. I agreed to meet him so that he could get into the garage to adjust the base. Once there I decided not to go back to work and went to bed to catch up on some much-needed sleep. Of course, my mind wouldn't turn off. The words echoed from the recesses of my mind. While there, I gathered some strength and mentally mapped out a plan. I waited for my primary physician to call me, which he did later in the evening. We made plans and he told me that the earliest he could get me in to see the surgeon was next Wednesday. Today was Thursday. He made several suggestions and asked if I needed something to relax. I said, "No," . . . and later agreed to a sleeping prescription. "I want a second opinion no matter what the surgeon says."

"You are entitled to that," said my doctor.

I thought I should lay out all of the plans, review my insurance arrangements, and consider all of the possibilities including death. I then put my funeral arrangements on my computer as a way of keeping busy, doing something meaningful and sparing my son the awful task of having to take care of that one morbid detail. However, I would leave it to him to modify it. Of course, planning the funeral may be another one of life's lessons. I just requested that he make it a musical memorial rather than a traditional funeral and that it be held in a pleasant and attractive setting.

Somehow, the future didn't seem so devastating. I think I tapped into that wellspring of hope and analyzed what had happened. It was a very small polyp and probably hadn't spread. Whatever, life wouldn't be the same possibly, but I was not going to give up even though my condition may be serious, I would fight for survival. Well, by now I feel better and have decided what the priorities are: contained and no spread, resection with no colostomy . . . In the interim, I would call some medical friends I know and friends who know the appropriate specialists and ask their advice. I would consult with an attorney friend and not my brother, an attorney, at this time regarding the best strategy for work and any leave, sick or otherwise that I may need, etc. Consulting with my brother would be like having to deal with my mom. I would tell my son first and then my family at a family meeting following the visit with the surgeon.

Thus began my journey down the road to drastic surgery and recuperation. First, I would get second and third opinions from those rated at the top of their field, colorectal surgery. My sister, Doby, had the contacts in New York and knew just the right official to get me to Memorial Sloan-Kettering right away. I figured that after that consultation, I would find a way to get into the best facility nearest my home and with the surgeon recommended by one of the field's most highly recognized surgeons at Memorial Sloan-Kettering. One of the surgeons he recommended was Dr. Shibata which we arrived at through a process of elimination. He was located at Moffitt Cancer Center in Tampa, Florida. Now, the trick was to gain immediate entry to Moffitt and to a consultation with Dr. Shibata. Luckily, I knew just who to call: Betty Castor and Sam Bell. Of course, they followed through.

Immediately after the diagnosis, not only did I research doctors and other experts, I went online and retrieved an extensive array of information regarding colon cancer and placed it in a notebook. I took the notebook with my comments and questions highlighted to my first consultation. I used those resources to assist me in seeking information from my doctor. During that first consultation with Dr. Shibata, I made it clear that if he could not resection my colon, to close me up and let me go out whole.

The surgery was successful and after two weeks in the hospital I was released to go home but was scheduled to go back every three months for the first year and then at six-month intervals, etc. Instead of going home, my son checked me into a nearby hotel because we were both afraid that something could go wrong in the next few days and that if it did, I would be too far away to get immediate attention from the doctor and staff that I trusted.

The Moffitt Center is a wonderful, attractive, pleasant and supportive environment. If one must have cancer, I would recommend that you choose not only the doctor carefully but the facility for surgery and recuperation. Like the Moffitt, it should be aesthetically pleasing and comfortable. At least for me it was comforting to be in a place of beauty, order and cleanliness to support my healing. From the cello players and the artists who visited to see if I was interested in listening or seeing or doing art, there was much that was inviting. You could even befriend a dog and seek his companionship. The room was large with a wall of windows to let in the sunshine and to look out at the beautiful landscape. It also accommodated a bed for my sister and later my son to sleep nearby.

Having a large family, many friends, and acquaintances, who visited, made the stay even more comforting. My room literally looked like an overstuffed florists. My friends and especially some of my Link friends sent some of the most beautiful arrangements I have ever seen. All of the staff and everybody who came to visit commented on the beautiful flowers and that I must be special because they just kept coming. My family was all there for the surgery along with my friends the Bryant's. My mom and youngest sister stayed for another week. My son came and stayed the second week and took me to a nearby hotel following my discharge from the hospital and then home. He even stayed at home with me for an additional two weeks tending my every need and supporting my recuperative efforts. The following week he had an assignment in Tallahassee and was therefore, with me most evenings. I felt blessed to have such a caring and wonderful son and family.

Through it all I was blessed that the surgery was successful and that I didn't have to have chemotherapy or radiation. But it is times such as these that cause one to ponder the essence of life and to recognize the important things and people in life. I am clear on these counts. I know what is important and what my purpose in life is. And, I will live life to meet that purpose.

## What Would I Do If I had Another Chance at Life?

If my life was threatened and I had another chance at life, wow! I would find a way to spend my time doing what I could to improve the human condition. I'd select a project that matters and could make a difference for those who are in need. I just hadn't narrowed it down. In the grander scheme of things I want to go to Western Africa or even back to Tanzania or South Africa and make helping one family or small group my mission in life. I will get in touch with Pete and Charlotte who are located just outside of Arusha, Tanzania and see if there is any way I can help with their mission. Given another chance I would do just that and make life more bearable and the future real for some impoverished children.

Here at home I am haunted by homeless children; homeless because their parent or parents are homeless; by generations of misguided youth who never learned because their parents never learned and therefore, could not teach them the values so essential to the "good" life. These values: responsibility, honesty, love and caring for others, sharing, resilience, persistence, tenacity, commitment, hard work, can yield positive benefits and a sense of accomplishment, yet they lack the ability to develop on their own or live vicariously to adopt them. What is the best environment in which to develop these young people? What are the ingredients for their development to be fruitful? Can they be saved? We have already lost a generation or two of our young black boys and many of our girls. Can't we do better? How can we ignore the travesty of lost souls and unproductive citizens? The answers are, yes we can do better and we can't ignore them! We mustn't!

As an aside, I would do the travel I had already planned to the Panama Canal area and on to the countries of Central America with major emphasis on Costa Rica, Nicaragua, Ecuador and Honduras; the Far East with emphasis on China, Egypt and India. I'd take a cruise through the Mediterranean and other spots as they come to me. I want to see more of the world, how others live and to experience their cultures and discern what makes them who they are.

However, my most important tasks would be to grab hold of those I have already helped and facilitate their helping others.

# You Jus Hav to be Der

You caint tell nobody 'bout dey's troubles if you ain't been der
You gotta be der to know what it is and what it's like
If you ain't been to de ocean, what you know 'bout dat?
Is der sand, is the water salty, is der breezes?
Is it hot? Is it cold? Is the sun beaming?

Whatcha know 'bout somebody else's troubles is whatcha dun been through yo'self

"I'se knows how ya feel" dun mean nutin if you'se ain't felt what I'm feeling.

I repeat here what a wise old lady from Palmetto back in the old days said when I was a youngster. These may not be the exact words but the message has stuck with me and the vernacular is hers.

# The Wind I

The wind blows and takes away the dirt
That's nature's way of cleaning the air.
Why not a wind for the mind that sweeps
It clean and rain that washes it down
Leaving in their path a mint of enthusiasm,
A burst of creativity, renewed optimism,
A vision of hope and images of solutions and faith in one's self?

# The Wind II

What are we to do when on the west bank we stand
While they are on the east bank?
The wind blows from the west
And moves us closer east.
The same wind carries them farther east.
Separate we were, separate we remain.

Is there a wind that blows two ways concurrently?
Can the east wind blow them west and the west wind blow us east?
Then we could move toward and not away from each other's positions.
Would that mean our thoughts would merge?
And what of our hearts?
Could we possibly be closer in our positions and coexist peacefully?

# Celebrating Family

# A Beautiful Day to Remember

And a beautiful day to remember . . .
That day on June 24, 1967
Your infamous night out with the boys
My first return from Chicago to meet you in Hendersonville
Our first-owned home

January 23, 1974
Russell's birth and our living vow to love and protect him. And to help him to become a good man. Our friends who throughout the years proved true And sustained us and brought life and light into our lives Our move to Daytona The rainfall, clouds, and thunderstorms that helped us to appreciate the sunshine, to grow in understanding of ourselves and each other and to feed our love.

A beautiful day to tell you my heart remembers all the joys and the touch of your love in my life . . . . Happy Anniversary . . .

Love, Your Altha

# A Birthday Wish for Aunt Eleanor

May your birthday be reminiscent of all that is good

The sunshine, the rain that washes away the sorrows,

The love of family and friends,

The saving grace of God,

Your moments of laughter,

Your wedding day, the birth of your children,

The blossoms and flowers of spring,

The kaleidoscope of leaves in the fall, and

The beach on a sunny day.

And, may your dreams replay your favorite tunes,

Your favorite times and star your favorite people, and

May you also find these treasures at the end of the rainbow!

# Christmas 2006

**My Dearest Russell,**

My, what a fine young man you are! I am always amazed at your sensitivity to others, your depth of understanding of the human condition, your ability to reach out and touch almost anybody of any station in life, and your willingness to help others who are less fortunate than you. You are articulate, intelligent, knowledgeable, and interested in issues and affairs around you locally, regionally, and in the world. You easily slip from local and personal issues to world affairs and you are informed on both. Well, at least you have an informed opinion on them all (smile).

Though we don't always agree, I admire your ability to discuss issues without getting too vested and to allow differences and disagreements to easily slide from view and your concern. You get along with almost anybody and can relate to all. You continue to be well read, interested in world affairs, and an interesting character.

But you know when I am most proud? It is when my friends who are aging now call and say, "Russell called me today" or "Russell stopped by." They are so pleased and so complimentary of you. They can't believe that you remember them and call to check in, visit them, and express your concern for their well-being. They all say, Morris and Jodie, Emmie, Vea, Lonnie and Alma, Robert and Ellen, Carolyn and Burt, Clara and Robert, Alba, Larry, Mrs. Estaras, Mrs. Johnson (before she became disoriented), Mrs. Thomas before her sickness and subsequent death, that "Russell remembers us old folk. He is the only young person who does." So many of them say that you are more concerned than their own children or other young relatives. They adore you! Your grandma, aunts, and uncles echo these sentiments.

I wish for you this Christmas season, and on the eve of the New Year of 2007, that you find satisfaction and happiness in your personal life, work and that you find time to enjoy life along the way. Of course, I know that you "smell the proverbial roses." Your and Karenna's trip to Alaska, going to the movies, going to exhibits and museums, the park, and all that you do to "just have fun" help to shape a mellow and calm George Russell Manning, II.

While you are an extraordinary human being, I know that you need to move on. You are doing OK and I am proud of what you are doing but you have so very much to offer that is not currently being tapped. I wish for you in 2007 that you will seek additional training and pursue a terminal degree that advances you professionally. Or that you will branch out on your own in this or another field that will bring you the satisfaction of achievement while affording a lifestyle with which you can be comfortable. Please do not allow yourself to get "stuck" in the position and place where you currently are. Even if you have to just move about, do so to get additional experiences, those that prepare you for management and leadership in the future. Of course, I will always be there to assist where I can even though you are not one to seek or take much help. Just know as I know you do, that I am willing to do so.

Lastly, I wish for you happiness found only in the mutual love of a special mate. It may not be now but sometime in the future. I do not wish to rush you only to say that that is my dream for you. I hope that when that special day does come, that you have selected someone who finds you as lovable and loving as you find her. Mutual love is the key to longevity in a relationship. We can discuss later what true and mutual love is but to sum it up, it is how that person makes you feel about yourself and how you make her feel about herself not just when you are together, but all the time. That's a long discussion and the manifestation of which I hope you spent twenty-six years observing.

Take care, my love, and keep on being the young man who makes everybody's heart sing.

My heart is hopeful and sings for you, George Russell.

Love, Mom

*Note*: Russell and Karenna recently married and their love is evident. I wish them a life of enduring love and happiness.

# Happy Birthday, Russell!

January 23, 2005

My, how time flies when you're having fun and in love!
It's hard to believe that thirty-one years have passed since that glorious day your dad and I went to High Point Memorial Hospital to deliver our bundle of joy—you.

I remember him saying the night before that I had taken some of the joy out of it because I had your delivery scheduled. I did that so that the doctor I had faith in could deliver you. He had planned a trip to Israel and was not scheduled to be in town for your projected time of arrival. I said to him, "You are going to deliver this baby! So tell me what we can do to make that happen."

Preceding my pregnancy with you, I had had a very difficult time with an ectopic pregnancy, which nearly ended my life. It erupted after four months of being treated for a severe infection, rather than the ectopic pregnancy, which did in fact infect my whole system, hospitalizing me for weeks and wreaking havoc on all of my systems. The doctors said that I would never have another pregnancy, and so they didn't believe I was pregnant with you. Only after this doctor, Crawford, and Dr. Brickler and cousin Blondell, here in Tallahassee, who did the test, confirmed unconditionally that I was truly pregnant, did the team there accept my pregnancy and begin to treat me accordingly. I came home to doctors, Brickler and Anderson, at the urging of Blondell to make sure I was going to be OK. Even so, the doctors in High Point, except Dr. Robert Crawford, just assumed that I would naturally abort, but as I developed, and they did their homework, and their jobs as obstetricians and gynecologists, they applauded the pregnancy.

But they didn't know you. You came into this world, planned, loved, and highly anticipated. We wanted you, and it was you who provided the glue to make us a true family. You were forceful but gentle and loving. Your smile lighted up our world.

I have never seen another human being so proud to be a father. However, I had to make him go to child-birthing classes, and at the first class when they showed the film of a real birth, he nearly passed out and left the room. I followed him, and he said, "I am not coming back to another one of these classes. That is gross!"

I immediately said, "If you don't, I won't have this baby!"

He looked at me at nearly eight months pregnant and laughed uncontrollably. I reminded him that he only had to be there and observe. I was the one actually doing the work. Needless to say, he got the courage to go back and finish the course, and was right there in the delivery room and actually helped deliver you.

Looking in the mirror set up for my viewing, I kept asking, "What is it?" Both he and Doctor Crawford, along with your godfather, Tillman, a doctor who attended the birthing, would say in unison, "We can't tell from the tip of the head." And then, "Oh, it's got a beautiful head of hair!" and then, from the head and later from the shoulders, the arms, and then came the cry, "It's a boy!" I was in a slow-motion movie. It was surreal. You were emerging bit by bit, slowly making your entrance into a world of joy, happiness, love, and warmth.

It was a cold January, but you lit a fire that penetrated the hearts and souls of those who came to know you. It was snowing, and when we took you home three days later, there was still snow on the ground. Your dad made a snowball for you and tried to pretend you were throwing it to or at him. He laughed as he fast-forwarded to the days to come when that would be true.

Even before you were born, we planned for you and later with you. Your dad began his savings plan for you the day the pregnancy was confirmed. So when I got back to High Point from a business trip, he showed me the savings account he had started. And as you know, there was more to come. You were to have everything that you needed but not be spoiled. We would love you unconditionally but be disciplined in ensuring that you had the principles and qualities of not only love but love coupled with discipline, responsibility, respect for yourself and others, a firm foundation in the church (from day one, you never missed a Sunday nor any special event), a thirst for learning and openness to new ideas, new thoughts, places, and a willingness to venture beyond the comfortable. All of this, and order in your life and the feeling of comfort that you had a home to come home to and the knowledge that no obstacle would be too great to overcome, that we would stand with you and, if necessary, for you.

You had a way of having your way even as an infant and throughout the years. The days in Daytona when we again had a split floor plan house, your dad decreed that you would not sleep in our bed. You'd always start there, and he would carry you off to your room at the other end of the house. Well, you'd beat him back to the bed by coming through the sun room to our bedroom. He finally gave up and simply tucked you in, although he'd occasionally maneuver again to get you to stay in your bedroom. You were never disrespectful, but you had your way of getting us to see your point of view, which would from time to time differ from our own. We were careful to always include you in our discussions on almost any topic: the world, politics, social issues, money, religion, etc. We read the paper and viewed news programs, and so did you. I think that sometimes others didn't understand that we valued your participation in our discussions as much as some other adults. You, at times, discerned the differences we had on issues, but you also came to appreciate our living our differences without hatred and disrespect.

You made us proud by the person you became. So often people overlook the truly important things in life but your dad and I always focused on those for you. You are a testimony to the best that there is in humankind. I hope that the world can one day see the man you are and truly value you and what you have to offer. More importantly, I hope that you will offer to the world your gifts and talents and that you freely share them. The world needs you and others like you to make this a better place for the oppressed, to lift the poor from poverty, to help our children and youth know the true value of an education, and seek out the best there is in humanity.

Son, I am proud of you and know that your blossom will continue to unfold in the years to come. Have a *happy birthday, Russell!*

Love, Mom

# Happy Thanksgiving

On this day of Thanksgiving, may we celebrate our fortunes:

**Family**—ours, others, and our ability and the opportunity to reach out and touch them;

**Love**—its' beauty, strength, and sustaining power;

**Friendship**—its' comfort, solace, familiarity, and those whom we call "friends";

Our **health and wellness** whatever its' state that has kept us present to observe another day and reunion with our loved ones;

The *opportunity* to *pledge* to ourselves that we will *achieve* and *preserve* the health and wellness of the greatest machinery known to mankind, the temple that is ours;

The **ability to see and smell** the unfolding of the rose blossom;

The *beauty* of nature's fall palette;

The **opportunity to hear** the song of birds, and to observe their beauty;

To **hold the hand of a young one** to steady his/her learning to walk and to **lend a hand to an elder** as her/his strength wanes from once steady and stern upright steps;

To **share our wealth and treasures** with those less fortunate, and help them to stand on their own;

From this day forward, may we "see" the world in all its beauty and strive to bring balance to our lives and . . . be thankful.

# Russell's Dad's Birthday

Did you remember yesterday? That's why you kept calling me I suppose. He would laugh at me because I did my usual; forgot his birthday. I can't help thinking of him now and missing him and wishing life had continued here on earth for him, me, you and us. We made a perfect family.

I have so many fond memories of our time together and especially the time with you. You completed us. He was absolutely the proudest dad I have ever known. Truly, no man has ever loved, cared for, nurtured and supported a baby, son and young man like your father. I don't think you ever participated in anything that he didn't attend. Do you remember the basketball, swimming, soccer, stickball, baseball, football, drama—Finian's Rainbow, the PTA festivals and meetings, meetings with teachers, You have a real human model to pattern your life after—a decent, honest, feeling, committed, loving, disciplined, firm but gentle, loving, supportive young man, husband and father.

When you were a baby and toddler, I hired a nanny against his wishes because I traveled frequently in my job and wanted to be sure that someone would be there to take care of you in my absence and while he was working. He argued that he didn't need anybody there in the evenings; that, "I can take care of my baby by myself!" I knew that he would have to attend evening meetings and didn't want to rely on him getting different people to babysit. The nanny, Mrs. Kelly, an older woman who had no children of her own, took you as her very own. She was wonderful, very caring and protective of you. Sometimes she wouldn't let the neighborhood kids in the house to play with you, except for Tammy and Chip Tillman who'd stop by after school to play with the "baby", their god brother. She even disobeyed your Dad when he would tell her she could go home for the evening and come back the next morning. She'd stay anyway. That would upset him. But they managed to co-exist and eventually learned to appreciate each other.

He waited until he found just the right girl to take home to his parents and to marry her. I know that he cherished me, our relationship and who we were together. He wanted so much for you and gave all he had to ensure

*Slices of Life* | 51

that you got it. I think he knows that you got it! He often said that you were a fine young man and that you were going to be a fine man! He only worried about your weight and what that would mean for your health and longevity.

I know that you will be just the man he had hoped—a fine son, husband and father among the many other roles you already play for your various relatives. You have become the glue for the families.

Thanks Russell for being who you are.

I love you . . . Mom.

# Russell's Valentine . . . 2003

Dear Russ,

I'll always be there with you and for you if you're serious and trying. Even after I'm gone, I hope you'll sense my presence and support and that you will have that quiet, still voice to guide you to reach and achieve; to always think of others less fortunate; to never just settle; and to find peace and love within and around you.

I hope your valentine's day was great! As usual, you were in my thoughts and prayers.

Love always,

Mom.

# Christmas 2004 and Before for the Flowers Family

A Letter to Ma'Dear and my siblings

"'Tis the Season to be jolly," the old saying and song go.

I hope that this Christmas finds you happy, healthy and filled with hope for the future. Who knows what that future will be? Consider the tremendous changes we have witnessed in your fifty-plus Christmases. Remember the one toilet/bathroom house shared by eight of us with Bea and Da'Doby hogging it, but mostly Bea? Remember that the sink and toilet knew when Christmas was because it stopped up every year and under the house I went with Da'Doby to fix them and I'm sure others followed after me. Of course, the extended use probably clogged a system designed for only moderate use. Every time it freezes as it is threatening to do today and tomorrow, I remember wrapping the pipes and even so, they froze and burst. It was just a part of life in Tallahassee at 1222 Ford Street.

Do you remember the festive and elaborate dinners for holidays, especially for Christmas? The table was set for all of us and as we grew up and joined with boyfriends and girlfriends and prospective mates, they too joined us around the table. There was, of course, the family prayer with all heads bowed and nobody even beginning to eat before Da'Doby sat down and gave us permission to begin. Of course, while heads were bowed, someone was sure to pop a morsel or two in her mouth.

The meals were the best there were to be had anywhere. We ate well and lots of it too! The traditional turkey, a big one, a big ham too with lima beans, greens, usually collards, mustards and turnips; macaroni and cheese, rice, candied yams, green beans, potato salad, carrot, raisin and pineapple salad with walnuts; ambrosia, regular and cracklin' corn bread, and hot freshly-baked yummy rolls that melted in your mouth; maybe a roast, chitlins sometimes, a possum or raccoon or even a rabbit but something wild, maybe squirrel or deer. It had to be something Da'Doby had hunted in the early days, and later something one of his friends had shot. As our numbers grew, the display of food and people spilled over into the kitchen and back/family room. We ate and talked, and ate and talked. By the end of the dinner somebody had probably gotten mad! And Da'Doby was probably the culprit. Ma'Dear generally tried to smooth rough feathers but was busy making sure we enjoyed every serving.

Now, the desserts were nothing to sneeze at: coconut cake with seven-minute frosting, german chocolate cake, pound cake, chocolate cake, and light and dark fruit cakes, sweet potato pies, apple pies, blackberry cobbler or "dooby" (I've never seen this written); a cream pie, lemon pies, brownies, cookies of all sorts of what was left after we nibbled and ate them right from the oven.

Somebody outside of our family probably can't imagine what the food was like. And anybody who happened to be there to see would always come back and make sure they were there when the next holiday came around. So friends of six Flowers children frequently dropped by for dinner and especially dessert. No bakery I have ever seen would have the array of desserts we had and they were all homemade and scrumptious. In fact, everything was homemade! Guess what? Now that I think about it, there is no buffet in town or anywhere that can rival our ole Christmas table and festive array of foods.

So much that we did was around the table. Dinner was a family affair, at least when y'all were little and everyone had to be there before anyone could eat. That put pressure on whoever thought about being late to be there 'cause the rest of us would get revenge if Da'Doby or Ma'Dear didn't get to them first.

Although I have emphasized the Xmas meal, the Xmas tree, and the living room and the family room that housed it were filled to the brim with everything we wanted. That means toys for six children! We got books, clothing, and other goodies. Every child had his own bicycle or tricycle, and, of course, skates depending on his or her stage of development. We all got a pair of Sunday shoes and a pair of school shoes and the same was true for clothing except each of us got more than the two outfits, and my mom made most of them.

However, that ole big dining room table should have been saved for eternity. If it wasn't serving up good food, it was the accountant's bale for paying the monthly bills; the homework unit for study and God forbid a homework session with Da'Doby. I suppose most of my siblings did what I learned early to do, make up homework if you didn't have any. Because anything you got from school was a heck of a lot easier than what Professor Flowers would give you. And he hovered over you to boot so that you became a fumbling, babbling idiot! And if you didn't think you were one he'd call you one. The memory of him and Junior doing lessons lingers in my brain and has a permanent resting place there.

Remember Da'Doby coming home every day during the holidays loaded with gifts from his mail customers? Boy! It was good to see him and search through all the goodies. Those were the days when people gave the postman and paper boy gifts and money. I still do. I especially respect the mailman even though today's technology has made it easier for them, they still have their challenges. I am sure there is some remnant of racism left but it is a bit more covert. In Da'Doby's day it was not only overt but rampant and nearly overwhelming! Can you now imagine that someone would leave the teaching and "principalship" to become a mailman because he could make more money, much-needed money to support his growing family? That is what our Dad did.

Remember Ma'Dear going to work as a teacher and coming home and cooking, ironing, cleaning, doing the laundry, getting us ready for whatever because we were always involved in something. Then, after everybody was settled, she sewed and made most of our clothes, even the boys! What a machine she was. I don't think they make mommas like that anymore! Of course, we all took our places and especially the older and younger two helped out. I don't know just how Fred and Doby Lee escaped cooking but they did. The tale goes that Da'Doby declared that he was tired by the time Doby Lee came along and said, "I'm tired of being a guinea pig. Let her husband teach her to cook!" I suspect that with Fred, Bea and I just continued to do the work. Back then, he was the first and only boy and a little pampered. But, by the time Junior and Ralph, the last ones, came along we had all hardened up. They learned to survive, they cooked, ironed, and did everything else.

Remember Junior hiding his money. He could always squirrel away his money. He was born stingy and thrifty. Then Ralph, the big spender and charitable brother would come along and discover his hiding places and have some fun with his friends. He would also do Fred in. Fred thought he was not making any money off his paper route. Only years later did Ralph confess that he had found his hiding place and routinely robbed his nest of his profits.

Remember doing those term papers on the dining room table with the manual typewriter? Remember the purple copy paper that you had to put between the sheets to make a copy? That was a messy deal! I was always messy anyway so there were erasures everywhere. Remember doing the research at home? We had what some kids referred to as a library because our parents and grandma loved books. And we always had the latest version of the World Book Encyclopedias and Britannica. I laughed when one of y'alls friends referred to us as having a library. That's where they too came to do their homework at least until Da'Doby started "helping," then they all found an excuse to go home.

Report card time was either a happy time or a killing time. If you had good grades, meaning all A's and maybe a B or two, you were in good stead. A C was not acceptable and you didn't see the light of day for the next six weeks. You never studied so hard to get off restrictions. But nothing could erase the butt whipping you got if you got a D or F, Whew! That only applied to Junior and Ralph. Ralph because he was always trying to live down the Flowers reputation and show that he didn't care about stuff like school and Junior because he was a slow starter and probably dyslexic or had another learning disability. But Da'Doby didn't know that then and Junior had a sore butt for years. Only later did he blossom and was probably the smartest one of us making stellar grades in college.

Remember, when Junior didn't pass the high school test so he couldn't get into college? Well, MaDear wasn't gonna have one of her children not go to college. Mrs. Estaras, a friend and Junior's English teacher who also taught my Mom and several other Flowers children was the first to recognize Junior's potential and shared her views with my Mom. My Mom had faith in Junior so she arranged for Junior to prepare for and pass the test so that he could go to college.

The summer before he entered college, my Mom hired Dr. Marshall to work with him but mostly to improve his reading skills; she identified his learning disability and continued to work with him through his first semester and he really blossomed. With the help given him by Dr. Marshall, Junior exceeded all expectations. In college, he went from nearly flunking in high school to nearly all As. But it was Mrs. Estaras who first recognized that he had tremendous potential. Just goes to show you what can happen with kids and how a loving, supportive and confident parent and/or teacher can make a difference or anyone for that matter.

Remember Bea's award-winning poem? I love that! She has always been so artistic. I think she has only skirted the issue and missed her professional calling. "Bea, I wish I had your talent." She was the high school queen, Miss Lincoln High and could design and make anything. I couldn't believe How she decorated and made stuff. The first time I ever saw cloth blinds they were designed and made by Bea for Doby Lee's Boca Raton home. She made the bed coverings and everything else. Bea produced the first grandchild offspring and he became the family's baby along with his brother who followed him. She could have been the Martha Stewart of her day.

Bea also had a penchant for orderliness and cleanliness. Well, too bad, she had to be paired with her little sister who was at the other extreme of order. While Doby Lee gathered junk and kept the room messy and junky, you could hardly find your way in it. One day when I was getting on them about making the bed, Bea said, "I made up my half; she's got to make her half!" Bea hated animals; Doby Lee loved them and rescued every stray she ever found. She'd bring home a stray dog or cat and Bea would see to it that the animal got hauled off never to return again. Plus, Doby Lee wanted the animal in the house and in the bed. Bea wasn't having any of that! Eventually, Doby Lee inherited my bed and room so that they each had their own space.

Bea also had this penchant for taking things apart. I remember, probably my second Christmas in Tallahassee. I got the housekeeping stuff like a real working stove and oven which I still have today, an ironing board and a working iron, a washing machine and all the trappings to go with it. I got several dolls and lots of clothes. While my eyes were off Bea, she took my stove and the iron and ironing board apart. She was always taking stuff apart and trying to put it back together, most times unsuccessfully. You'd sit in a seat and fall to the floor because the screws were missing. I suppose she got that from Da'Doby who was notorious for breaking our new stuff. I remember when we got this new motorola combination. It was a fine piece of furniture. Da'Doby claimed he could take it apart and put it back together. Well, it never worked again and it was brand new! Of course, Bea was super smart just like him and an Nearly an all A student.

Doby Lee too is logical and creative. She writes and organizes well. She is a supportive sister and a family rock. She made her parents glad and proud so many times, so many successes: integrating Leon and surviving. Although she wasn't in the first group to graduate, she went as a sophomore and, of course, graduated later; her winning the Miss FSU as the first black queen at a predominantly white university made national news; she became the Commissioner of the Human Resources Administration for the city of New York, the largest agency of its type in the world; an executive at WR Grace, Inc. And she returned to the area, purchased a house in Thomasville as a bed and business retreat. Now to our delight she is with her idol, Fred, managing his law firm. Since they both know everything, it's amazing that anybody else can survive in there.

Ralph, the youngest, is billed as the comedian of the family and can really make you laugh about almost any situation. Underneath that funnyman veneer, lays a soft-hearted disciplined and very smart man. But from day one he didn't want to study. He used to say, "Y'all hold up the brains in the family. I ain't trying to make all As, just enough to keep Da'Doby and Ma'Dear off my butt." Ralph always talked about how Da'Doby was the first terrorist. Mostly how he terrorized us kids. Everybody was afraid of him including our friends. If you're scared, I guess you would be more likely to toe the line but that didn't always work. Even knowing a whipping was in the making, or severe punishment like not being able to do anything for six weeks, Ralph and Junior would drink some of Da'Doby's liquor and refill the bottle with water. One night when they thought he was in the bedroom asleep, he laid in wait for them and Caught them drinking the liquor and refilling the bottle with water. Well, there was hell for them to pay.

We were taught to look out for each other. My brother Junior was following through on what he was taught one day as he saw several boys ganging up on his younger brother, Ralph. Knowing that he is supposed to look out for his brother, he tried to help him out. However, as the gang began tussling with Junior, Ralph got loose and ran for home, leaving Junior to fend for himself. When Junior got home, he was dusty from wallowing on the ground, his clothes torn, and he was bruised. He started at Ralph as MaDear caught him and asked what had happened. MaDear reprimanded Ralph as Junior swore that he would never help him again. MaDear told him that he had better but that Ralph was never to leave him stranded again. Ralph said in his usual laissez faire way, "Wut'nt no need for both of us to get beat up!" She had to laugh at that.

Fred too is logical and loves all things natural; plants and gardens, but is very focused. Remember Fred and his "lock on" aloe? If you had a cold, a headache, stomach ache, or anything wrong with you, aloe could heal you and he grew it plentifully. Of course, he used it for its healing powers. Then one day, he had chest pains and his wife, Loretta rushed him to the hospital thinking he was having a heart attack. Nobody wanted to tell Da'Doby that his star son had had a heart attack and was at the hospital but we finally broke down and told him. We thought he was gonna have a heart attack himself but he calmed down and asked, "What happened to his aloe?"

Fred was one of the early integrators of FSU and the first black athlete scholar, receiving both academic and athletic scholarships from the university. He was a star pitcher at FSU, who was recruited by the St. Louis Cardinals out of high school. To our parents, it was unthinkable that he would not go to college. However, he only received playing time when the team was in trouble. He, of course, suffered the indignities that accompanied blacks who entered the world of predominantly white universities. After a year and due to the extremely stressful situations, he gave up playing on the baseball team. He graduated with honors from FSU.

Later, he attended law school at the University of Florida. His graduation from Law School was probably one of our dad's crowning glories. He reveled in the achievement and had his old college mates, the Scotts from Madison there to celebrate with him (Ed Scott's parents). He was all smiles.

Do you remember the vegetable garden in the backyard and the back lot? We had greens, peas, beans, okra, tomatoes, bell pepper, and every vegetable you could name as well as corn, sugar cane, and peanuts. Of course, pecans were plentiful as well. I remember that ole wringer washing machine and Ralph being hardheaded when told to stop playing with it. Suddenly, his hand got caught in that wringer and it lifted him off the floor before we could stop it and rescue his arm. He still has the scar to show for it.

I was the big sister and I guess I did what big sisters do. Growing up, I loved my sisters and brothers as my own. I vowed that I would not have any other children because I had them and they were enough. I also remember secretly taking a job cleaning a house for a white couple so that my siblings could have an allowance. Every week when I got paid, I'd give them an allowance according to their ages, like from a dollar down. Bea got more because she was the oldest. When my dad found out, it was all over! He had never endorsed any of us working, especially in those kind of jobs because he thought that was demeaning for us and he wanted better for his children. However, his discovery meant that I got an allowance and so did my siblings.

When I left home, they were still kids and I felt obligated to buy for them especially for special occasions. I also wanted them to get some other experiences so when I came home we'd go out to eat. I'd take them on trips to visit me or to other places. And wherever I moved, I had them come and visit. On one such visit to Ocala, I was vacating and cleaning out my house for the summer. I left them at home while I ran an errand. They claimed they heard something and got scared. They ran for the closet but Junior beat them to it and locked them out. They were scared stiff and when I got back I admonished Junior for not protecting his siblings. He said, "Well, somebody had to live to tell about it. So, I figured I was the one." I could only laugh.

On another occasion I took them to the Sadler Hotel in Orlando (Black folks finest in the area). We had dinner downstairs in the restaurant. They all got to order off the menu and what they wanted. Junior ordered fried chicken. He went behind the counter and dragged a box by the side of the table. We didn't pay much attention because everybody was busy enjoying their meals but I couldn't help but notice as Junior began to put his bones in the box. With a shocked look and startled voice I admonished him, "Boy, put that box back. You are in a restaurant; you don't do that and use your manners!" By that time everybody else was looking and broke out into a laugh. Junior and Ralph didn't get the pressure in manners at the table as much as the rest of us. They were the "last of the Mohicans" as my mom and dad would say.

Talk about what my dad would say; those were precious proverbial jewels. I wish we had captured more of them for our children and grandchildren and the generations to come. I think our favorite and one everybody remembers is, "If I tell you a butterfly can plow, you'd better hitch him up!" This usually came in response to one of us getting one of his trivia, literature or historical questions wrong. We'd respond, "You think you know everything!" Another to the same response by us was, "I may not know everything but I know so much it's a damn shame," or "What I don't know you can put in a teaspoon." Well, my son reminded me upon my telling him what Da'Doby said, that today that would be the whole of man's knowledge on a computer chip.

He was an exceptionally intelligent man who loved books and newspapers. Even though we subscribed to the local newspaper, every Sunday of my young life, I had to go to Ashmore's drugstore to get the collection of newspapers that he read: The Washington Post, New York Times, Tampa Tribune, Miami Herald, Jacksonville Times Union, and the St. Pete Times (four or more of these). Occasionally, he wanted the Orlando Sentinel as well which along with the Jax paper he felt would give him the conservative perspective. I would be weighed down with papers on my bike. I think he made sure that I had a big basket on my bike so that I could carry those papers. Boy was I glad when I could drive legally! Driving made the Sunday morning trip before Sunday school much easier. Years later, I laughed as I assumed the habit.

Going to church every Sunday was a given. Since I had spent my earliest years with my maternal grandparents who were devout AMEs, it was unthinkable to me that I would go anywhere else but to an AME church. That was my connection with them. So, I made the trek to Bethel AME Church every Sunday while I was in town or if I was visiting my grandparents, I went to Turner Chapel AME with them. At first, Johnnie Blake who lived up the street from us walked me to church every Sunday. When we moved from Georgia St. where we lived with my grandmother to Ford Street in our own brand new house, I took the trek to Bethel every Sunday with my little sisters and brothers in tow. They later went to Bethel Baptist where my parents joined and our paternal great grandfather was one of the founders.

On Sunday afternoons I used to steal the car by backing it off the back lot without cranking it and pushing it a few yards down the street so that my dad wouldn't hear it. I knew that he slept every Sunday afternoon with his papers. So I'd slip and drive around for awhile. My brother, Ralph saw me one Sunday and said he was 'gonna tell. I bribed him by taking him for a ride. When I returned, he got out of the car and ran backwards saying he was 'gonna tell as I begged him not to. Needless to say, I met my punishment behind that one. I don't think I got to go anywhere for two months.

I'd also steal my mom's car while she was at school teaching since I attended the same school. Once I skipped a study hall and while working on a project, I had my then best friend, Laurestine to go with me downtown. While trying to parallel park, I ran into the parking meter and dented the passenger door of the car. Was I scared? We couldn't get it fixed so I drove back to the school and asked Mr. McCone, one of the teachers who taught auto mechanics, if he could save my life. He told me where to go and they simply took a big rubber hammer and knocked the door and fender back out smooth and you couldn't even tell it. What a relief!

Life in the ole house changed. I came home frequently while I was single and teaching in Ocala (for five years). On several occasions the changes were shocking and unwelcome to me while others were simply a sign of the times. One of the times when I came home, there sat Doby Lee in the living room with her boyfriend who was always around and that was a change. But I noticed that she had something on her legs. I thought that she was wearing paisley stockings but to my amazement, she had her legs painted. Now, that may not seem so odd to some, but in my house when I was growing up, I could not even wear red fingernail polish. It was the mark of "women of the street!" I couldn't wear regular stockings permissibly until my junior or senior year in school and only then on special occasions and Sundays. Of course, I'd slip a pair out and take with me to change before I got to wherever I was going. My dress length had to be just so and below the knees, nothing tight and seductive and my hair which was so thick that nobody wanted to do it, had to be in an "acceptable style." Bea, to some extent, experienced the same thing. However, Doby Lee always liked odd styles in everything! So, she broke the chain of conformity and dressed more like she wanted to which was more colorful and "hippy" styled at times. I asked my dad what was happening in the house and he said, "I guess I just got tired."

On another occasion I came home and Royal, the beloved first grandchild, was playing in the living room. He scratched the front screen over and over again. My dad who was watching him pleaded, (now that's a change, pleading with a child) "Baby, stop scratching on that screen." He did this over and over again. I stood there in awe that my dad who used to tell us something only once before he knocked us into the next day would beg and plead with a two-year-old to stop something. Royal didn't stop so my dad got up and left the room. Wow! I was speechless.

Then after I was married and living in Durham, North Carolina, I went home unannounced, arrived there and couldn't get in the house. The door was locked! When I was growing up, nobody knew where the key was and of course, it was never used. The door was always unlocked or open. Further, there was nobody there. I was absolutely shocked and thought there was always somebody in this house. It was never empty. The Landers, our next door neighbors, told me where the key was once they greeted, hugged me and welcomed me home. I went in and discovered another surprise: There were no pots on the stove and nothing cooked and waiting for me and anybody else to devour. I just sat down in amazement at these drastic changes and couldn't believe them.

Yes, ole Ford Street had changed. I guess I thought it would remain frozen in time. But like me and the kids, life had simply evolved and we moved with it. The younger siblings grew up in a different time and different household but the thread of order in life, celebrations of all kinds—every birthday was marked with elaborate celebrations and lots of gifts—Easter, Thanksgiving and Mother's and Father's days were as celebratory as Christmas. Anyone missing from the table was truly missed! The values from that ole house were deeply embedded in our psyche and of course, molded us into who we are.

I think we are indeed fortunate. We all have talent and are smart. We came from a stable home and though the times were occasionally tough, most didn't realize what tough really was.

Those were good ole days to remember. Times are different, more technologically grounded and the days of 1984 that George Orwell wrote about are here and beyond. We have a history to cherish, a solid foundation to stand on and a value-based compass to guide us into the future. And though the future as we anticipate it is uncertain and scary at times, I am certain we will survive it and carry on.

One thread of continuity will be the dinner table this Christmas and the discussions and laughter and merriment and maybe an argument or two. We always discuss politics, history, and literature like our parents always did with us. And, we can really get on each other. But at the dinner table, somebody's 'gonna see the situation differently and get mad. It won't last for long and we'll move on. My brother Ralph's wife, took us too seriously and said, "Y'all really kill each other off and attack each other. You don't act like you like each other." She didn't understand, we're used to it and are each other's harshest critics but we love each other to the core and will stand with each other through thick and thin until the end. Just let somebody outside talk about one of us or in any way try to harm one. They have a mighty army to ward off and it would be nearly impossible to win. I can't wait to eat and laugh and sleep and talk and talk and listen, and maybe get mad, etc.

Have a Merry Christmas and a promising New Year! Thanks for taking this trip down memory lane with me.

Your Daughter and Sis,
Altha

Cc: Son, nieces, nephews, and grands

# Epilogue

MaDear, who recently died, had a tremendous influence on me. Her commitment to her family and especially her children was incomparable. I cannot imagine another human being who is more devoted to her children than she was. Both she and my father made tremendous sacrifices to ensure that their children would be wholesome, law abiding, and successful children and adults. They believed that their children, their proper upbringing, academic skills, social attributes, and participation in appropriate activities were their purpose in life. We were their mission, and they would do anything to make sure that we had what we needed and more.

As we grew up, MaDear became more involved in civic activities and stressed the importance of us looking out for each other but also beyond ourselves to help others. She and my father, who died in 1987, demonstrated daily how we could make a difference. They did! So much of what is written here is but a fragment of the experiences they afforded.

# Lessons Learned

From, MaDear, Da'Doby, Granddaddy, and others
These pages recount just a few of the lessons I learned from my parents and grandfather.

*I learned that we should help those in need and that we are all humans; no one better than another no matter the person's circumstances*

I'm sure that I have heard those phrases repeated many times, but it is not the saying of the phrases that made an impact on me but the examples demonstrated throughout their daily lives that made a profound impact. My earliest memories of humanitarian efforts were of my granddaddy, Herbert Garrett Hadley, who was a farmer in Palmetto, Florida, delivering fresh vegetables that were his "seconds," or that he could not sell at the big market in Tampa that day, to needy people in the neighborhood. So every afternoon, following a full day (14 hours+) at the farm, and after taking his workers home, he made the deliveries of mostly vegetables of all kinds, and some fruits like strawberries, and melons.

My parents were also living examples of giving and helping others. When we moved to our new home on May 19, 1949, in Tallahassee, Florida, there were families that were in need of assistance. I don't know what governmental help was available to them but it was probably not as comprehensive as it is today. There was one family in particular of seven kids and a single mother that lived near us. The mother worked at night and the kids were left alone under the care of the oldest children. It appeared that she was not able to fully support the children. At the time, we had a vacant lot behind our house which faced the street behind us. My parents used our backyard and sometimes this lot for a garden. We grew just about all vegetables, sugarcane, and peanuts, and we had fruit and nut trees: persimmons, pears, plums, and pecans. The bounty from the garden was shared with the neighbors and especially this family.

However, when dinner time came along, MaDear would have the children come and eat with us, or send a bundle of food home for the older youth to set for the table, because most times the older ones would not come for meals. But most days the younger ones ate with us. On several occasions, Da'Doby complained about the cost of our groceries. Finally one day, he said to MaDear that he could not afford to feed the whole neighborhood; that the kids' mom would have to take care of them. She asked, "What if she can't?" He just shrugged and repeated that he could no longer afford it.

The next day when he came home and we were all seated around the dinner table, he asked where the kids were. MaDear replied, "You said that you couldn't afford to feed them." Da'Doby got up and instructed us to stop eating and sent one of my younger brothers to get them. He said, "I can't sit here and eat knowing that those kids may be hungry!" From that day forward there was no discussion regarding them eating with us or getting food gifts. He tried another tactic though: Shopping for the family himself. He scrutinized the list and revised it then took me to the grocery store with him. We followed the list my mom had prepared, and that he had revised. Well, when we got to the cash register to check out, the grocery bill was more than double what my mom usually spent. He just about died from the shock! Well, that cured his shopping and complaining about the cost of groceries. My mom had mastered the technique of getting lower cost items and those on sale. He, on the other hand always bought the top of the line. That's why I preferred him to take me shopping for clothing and shoes.

Years later, one of the boys from that family returned. He was in college in one of the Mid-Atlantic States. This tall, handsome, young man came to our house and without knocking, came on into the house, and asked where Mrs. Flowers was. We stared at him and reluctantly told him that she was in the back bedroom. He proceeded and went to her. She sat up startled, with just a sparkle of recognition. He said to her, "Mrs. Flowers, I had to see you and personally thank you for all that you did for me and my family." She asked reluctantly, "Are you Charles?" He replied, "Yes Ma'am."

As we all stood in the doorway, they embraced each other with tears rolling down their cheeks as she bombarded him with questions about his whereabouts, the other children, and his mom. She always asked about them, and we had heard that he and his older brother were both doing well.

He told her that he was in college on a scholarship and that he was doing well and expected to graduate the next June. She cried more, and said, "I knew you could do it." He proceeded to tell her about all of the other children and how they were faring. It was a great moment and one of the biggest payoffs for my mom. She never forgot that and neither did I. That one experience made an indelible mark on my heart and I'm sure on my brothers and sisters as well.

*Stand up for what you believe in even if you have to stand alone*

Following the crowd was never acceptable if the crowd was wrong. We were taught to think for ourselves, make decisions based on what is right and wrong, and not make excuses like, "Jennie was doing it," or "Joe said do it." I can recall that there was a young girl in the neighborhood who was severely disfigured and as is commonly the case; kids would make fun of her. MaDear who was a teacher, and sometimes walked to and from school, was late leaving school one day as some of us lollygagged along after school. She caught some kids making fun of the disfigured girl as I stood by, and of course, she taught us all a lesson. When I got home she asked me why I didn't defend the girl. I told her that I wasn't picking at her and felt sorry for her but didn't know what to do. She asked how I would feel if I had been that little girl and if I thought it was right to "pick" at other children for any reason. I said "no" because I was often the brunt of their mischievousness even though it was for different reasons (They thought I was the teacher's pet, although, I felt that teachers were harder on me). MaDear explored with me what I could do if this occurred again; like take the girl by the hand and declare her as my friend, tell her not to worry that they didn't know any better, and that she was a great person, and some other ideas which I have long forgotten. It wasn't the specific strategy that took hold there, but that I should stand up for someone less fortunate, or who is being picked on, because it is the right thing to do even in the face of difficulty. The difficulty for me would have been getting bullied even more and perhaps beaten.

I employed that same lesson with my son when he and his buddies were chatting about a kid who appeared ragged and generally unkempt. They thought it was funny and made a joke about him even to his face. After scolding all of them and demanding that they talk to their parents about it,

I insisted that they beg the little boy's pardon. After the other boys had left, I had a long discussion with Russell, my son. I think I helped him to see that he could make a difference with how the other boys treated the young man. That he could befriend him, because no matter, he was a human being worthy of respect just like himself. Several weeks later, Russell came to me and told me how sorry he was about how he and the other boys treated the boy. I asked what brought that on. He said that he had talked to him on several occasions, and that the young man finally told him that his father was in prison, and that his Mom was ill and could barely take care of them. He then asked if we could help him and his siblings. We discussed it with his dad and so the journey to redemption began. Clothing, toys, food, cash, and visits helped the young man see that he was not a prisoner of his situation. I was proud of Russell for caring and told him that I was so happy that he took a personal interest in the young man.

Of course, sometimes the lessons that we teach our children come back to bite us. After Russell went off to college, he called back one evening to say that he was occupying the President's office with a group of other students. On several occasions we had discussed events leading up to this occupation and I knew he was right in his indignation. However, my first reaction was, "Boy, I sent you off to college to get a college degree and not to get in trouble!" All I could think of was him failing his classes or getting put out of school and losing his scholarship. Of course, it would be on the news, and he was forewarning us in case they showed his photo. Before I could say anything else, he informed me that he was not going to miss out on his classes and any assignments, because he had taken care to carry his books and study materials to the office with him so that as they sat, they were also studying. After discussing it some more, we told him that if he felt that strongly about the issue that drove them to "take over" the President's office, we'd support him but he was to stay in close communication with us so that we could advise him and the group if things changed. We advised them to not destroy or bother anything and to keep the office clean. We hung up the phone and said, "Oh well, he is doing what we taught him to do."

This lesson in particular has been demonstrated time and again in my adult life. I learned to speak up when I see what I perceive to be a wrongheaded direction, decision, and action, and I don't mind being alone in my actions. Whether I am in the boardroom with policy makers, in a social group with friends, or observing strangers, I feel very uncomfortable allowing actions to occur that are detrimental to people, especially those whose voices are silenced by the "system."

Perhaps one of the most dynamic lessons taught by my Mother's Actions resulted from the events surrounding the closing of the Black High School, Lincoln, where she taught. Teachers from Lincoln were assigned to other predominantly White schools except her and possibly another teacher, Christine Knowles. The county school officials and other authorities were pressuring these two teachers because their children were among those integrating the premiere White school, Leon High School. Further, they knew that these two teachers were working with the Rev. C.K. Steele the chief activist leader of the integration movement in Tallahassee.

With Rev. Steele's and Christine's advice MaDear went to the Lively Vocational and Technical School every day without a class or room assignment. This went on for a year or more. Rev. Steele pointed out that the powers that be just assumed that she would get tired and disgusted and quit but that she should show up every day. They just didn't know Aldonia H. Flowers. She didn't quit, attended all of the faculty meetings and demanded that she receive an assignment and that her pay not be jeopardized. They eventually succumbed to the pressures and gave her a class assignment. Even though it was tough and stressful, she stuck to her principles and helped the system adapt and change. By the time this occurred, I had left home but stayed in touch daily. I felt the brunt of what they were doing to my Mom and resented it.

*Be respectful of the elderly*

Although I sensed it intellectually, at no time did this become more meaningful than when MaDear became frail and helpless. Even before that I suppose it was clear as I watched Granddaddy age and become frail. But I think that somewhere in between, I forgot the lesson I was supposed to remember and apply. As a child, I was my Granddaddy's heart, and he was mine. He was the first man to capture my heart solidly and totally. I frequently reflect on the old man walking while holding his little granddaughter's hand. I wish that the scene had been captured in a photo. However, as he aged and became more frail, my heart would always stop beating as I gazed at his slow shuffle, pale skin, and deepened wrinkles, and heard his weak voice which at one time had been both forceful and gentle.

On my last visit before he died, I asked him what I could get for him. He thought and then said, "Get me some slide-in bedroom shoes." The next weekend I didn't go to visit as I had promised. He died before I could get to him and give him the shoes. I stood by his bed holding the shoes in my hands while I cried my heart out. I wanted so much for him to see that I had gotten the shoes. I kept those slippers for ages, moving from place to place, as a reminder of Granddaddy. From that point on, every time I would see an elderly person struggle to walk or to perform even the most basic functions, I would instantly think of Granddaddy, and rush to the rescue if necessary. How I wish I could give him those slide-in bedroom shoes!

My mother's aging process and her subsequent illness were not always obvious to me, mostly because she had always been so strong, and seemed to be able to handle anything. My youngest sister and I would push her to do more than she probably felt capable of doing. But she knew how she was feeling even when some of the doctors would say the opposite. We believed the doctors and not always her. How I wish I could replay those frames in our lives, and give her the attention, and demonstration of love she so richly deserved and wanted.

I can see her eyes now searching for that demonstration of sympathy that I didn't always so readily give a hug or an "I love you." Although I would occasionally massage her weak legs, visit her several times a week, take her to the beauty parlor, to get a manicure and pedicure, prepare or take her to lunch or dinner on those outings, if given another chance, I would leap over the clouds to please her. As is often the case, I didn't know until it was too late that her days with me and my siblings were already numbered.

Today, just a glimpse of frailty, aging, or struggle will automatically prompt me to reach out to assist. I would walk slower with her rather than ahead of her. I would hold her hand and prop her up. I would sit for long hours to talk with her, and listen intently to her stories. I would not get aggravated when she told the stories over and over again, or made the same comment each time we passed certain properties. Only in the last months of her life did I realize that death was imminent. We talked for hours as I visited her in the rehab centers, and throughout the nights I spent with her in the hospital. We made up for some of the lost time of freely speaking and sharing but it was not enough. It never is!

Perhaps her legacy to me will be my sharpened sensitivities to the elderly I encounter . . . .

*If you make a bad decision and end up going the wrong way, make a U-turn*

Sometimes in life we make a decision that ends up being the wrong one. Yesterday as I hurried to go to a reception in honor of my sister-in-law, I intended to take a short cut but forgot that taking that route meant dealing with one-way streets and therefore, going several blocks out of the way. Sometimes life is also that way. We intend one thing but end up doing something different that takes us out of the way and takes a longer time to get to do what it is that we intend. When those times occur, I learned early on that the least desirable path may be longer and bumpier, but it can still get us there. Even though the detour is not necessarily the easiest and can cause us to stumble, fall or just give up, giving up does not get us where we want to go. It may take longer to get there, and we may be late as I was for the reception, but we can still get there. When those times occur, just take the detour or the longer way around, but stay focused on where you want to go.

Sometimes those bad decisions take the form of teen pregnancy, choosing to marry the wrong man or woman, dropping out of school, using drugs, abusing prescriptive medicines, staying in a bad relationship, being around people who are poisonous to our well-being, and a myriad of other situations. My MaDear and Da'Doby used to say, "Just because you made a mistake, it's not the end of the world. Everybody has struggles, challenges, and obstacles in their way, and they have even failed sometimes. It is how you handle these that define who you are. If you meet someone who hasn't had problems, or even failed at something, you have met a ghost who hasn't lived. Get up, dust yourself off, refocus, and keep going. You can do it!"

I remember one especially trying time in my life when I had entered and subsequently left a really bad relationship. Da'Doby surprised me and shielded me from the world. He even told a very strong and persistent aunt to back off and give me space so that I could begin to heal. He said to me, "Take your time so that you can get back on track." I return to their advice often. I thank my parents when I get in my solitude and figure out how to meet life's challenges or how to overcome something that has baffled me or derailed my plans. Never is my plan to give up.

How rewarding it is when you reach your destination in spite of the obstacles in your way. The challenges made it even more worthwhile and serve to "steel" your resolve to conquer the next challenge.

# Love

# What Is Love?

What is love? I think I am beginning to understand. It is a feeling that emanates from deep within and permeates your whole being. It can't be separated from the rest of you to be isolated, analyzed, reconfigured, or in any way tampered with. It just is. It is unconditional regard for, belief in, and trust of the object of your love. Even when you "see" the frailties and flaws, you still believe and have faith in him. You know that the good lies within, that there is a diamond in the rough and that the sun shines beyond the clouds. You grasp that perpetual rainbow and hold onto it with all your might. You believe with all your might in him, in love.

It rules the heart and the head without regard for the other. It manifests itself in something described as emotions, those ephemeral, surrealistic, smoky, or cloudy configurations that you just can't grasp, that float right through your fingers, escape your being like cold breath or smoke. Have you ever tried to grasp the smoke or fog in your hands? You see it, but you can't grasp it, hold it, control it, mold it, or make it conform to some standard of behavior you have set for yourself. It possesses you without being possessed, in your dreams both waking and in sleep. It drives you to despair, picks you up, holds you gently, tightly, and squeezes the life out. It is loving in return, gentle and harsh. It is controlling and yet freeing. It demands but gives.

It is love, a risk, a challenge, a heartache, a joy, a breath of delight. It is love!

# Love Is a Many-Splendored Thing

It's a breath of fresh air
It's a simple, knowing glance
It's being held by that special someone with no words necessary
It knowing that she will be there for you, no matter what
It's not having to say what you think, and knowing that she understands
It's the special touch that resonates throughout your psyche
It's having her back and knowing that she has yours
It's the memory of time together touching, holding, being held, and sweet conversations
It's relishing the sun, admiring the clouds, and enjoying the rain together
It's planting a garden, tending it, watching the flowers grow, and savoring their beauty and scents
It's wanting to satisfy her, and knowing that she wants the same for you
It's enjoying a ride through the woods together
It's enjoying silence together
It's feeling her print on your heart
It is knowing that she will forever love and cherish you
It's creating memories to retrieve when that is all that is left
It's you!

# An Ode to You

I want to be loved by you.
I need your love,
The touch of your hand,
The golden glint in your eyes,
The solemn, soft, and knowing smile,
Say that you too are wanting.

I watch your moves,
Every muscle toned,
Your clothing personifying all of you.
Your moves perfectly synchronized.
An air of distinction,
A flavor of urbanity,
Sophistication and intelligence,
Yet these are only reflections of you,
Genteel and gentle.

# Distractions

We went to dinner. Someone was playing the piano and my favorite singer, Pam Combs Laws, sang. The music was so sentimental that I could hardly stand it. All I could do was think of him, dream of him, and almost touch him. My friend thought that I was going back in time. Instead, I was in the now. Have you ever loved someone so much it hurt? I can't believe it even though I live it, see it, feel it, and know it is so; I'm still amazed by it.

Life is a wonder, a surprise, a disappointment, it is happy, sad, and yet it is life in its natural state. I guess love is like that too. I laugh, I cry, I hurt, and I yell out in ecstasy. He is my breath, the muscles that make me smile, he is with me, he is gone from me. He tells me he loves me and leaves me. He's here for a moment and he's gone. I can only share a few moments, just a few. There really is no room for me, no place, no space—just the clouds that disappear in the sunshine. So I acknowledge the truth and try to move on. I tell myself, just put one foot ahead of the other and you will move and eventually you will get there.

I hope so. I hope so.

# Do You Feel it?

Can you feel it? Don't you see it? Listen, you'll hear it.

The taste of sweet strawberries right off the vine, trickling through your soul brings a smile to your lips.

The aroma of a fresh spring day wafts through the air.

It is all encompassing.

Don't be afraid.

Bask in its glow. Be soothed by its rhythms,

Nurtured by its tenderness,

Support and understanding.

It is love, my dear—do you feel it?

# Fear of Loving

I think we're moving to another plane now.
There's less fear and guardedness, more openness (to loving)
You even acknowledge love.
You don't know what to do with it,
How to control it.
You love me—you withdraw and hide to keep
Your emotions intact—to control loving and my intrusions.

You can't believe it—that I do love you.
You can't trust me with your heart.
You're afraid and skeptical—that I'll not stick, nor stay,
That my love is tenuous.
"We'll see," you always say.
Indeed, we'll see!

# I Did It!

Today I did it!
Because you encouraged me
I proved that I could go for it,
Pull it all together
Because I knew you were in my corner.
The proposal lays ready for your review and approval
Because you wanted it for me.

I want and need your approval, your support,
Your understanding.
Because I can do anything with you on my side.
Because you reach across the miles,
Your touch lingers and
The sweet dew of your kiss
Reminds me that I am yours, and
I can do anything!

# I Dreamed of You

I dreamed of loving you.
I didn't know it would hurt so much.
Joy, pain, sorrow—
Inextricable dimensions of the
same element.

Surely as the sun shines, shadows of
darkness will fall.
Sweetness, tenderness, regrets and tears,
Imprint the moments.
Moments that last forever; Moments too short and bittersweet.

Eternal memories reflect pools of tenderness,
Passion, honesty and life's hard, cold realities.
It can't be—it's not real—it's only a
Moment in time, an eternity.

# I Love Your . . .

I love your lips when they're wet and sensuous
With wild desire.

I love your eyes when love
Lights them with passionate fire.

I love your arms when your warm dark flesh touches
Mine in a gentle embrace.

I love your hair when the
Strands sparkle and enmesh your kisses
Against my face.

# I Miss You

I miss you; I really, really miss you.
When there are clouds in the sky,
When the sun is bright and high,
When noises in the air push away the quiet still,
When moments of silence are buried in the till,
When the starlight twinkles in the night,
And when night fades away to a hopeful day of light.
I miss you!

# I Wish You Love

My hope is that
You will grow to trust me
And allow me to be at home in your heart.

May my roots go deep down
in your soul
and may you have the
power and the wisdom to understand

How wide,
How long, how high
And how deep my love
Really is!

May you experience the
Love that I give to you
Even though it is so profound
You will never fully
Understand it.

May you be filled
With my love and
Fill your life with love.

More than this,
I wish you
Joy and happiness
But most of all
I wish you
Love!

# I Wonder

I am wondering what created the distance.
Was it the miles between us
Or was it awareness that without physical closeness, distance is inevitable?
When we are apart, do we remember across the miles
the ecstasy?
Can we feel each other's pulse?
Hear each other's voice?
See each other's eyes?
Indeed, be each other?
When we are apart, why are we so reluctant to risk
An "I love you",
An "I miss you",
Or "I need you?"
I wonder if we wander.

# Impromptu Visit

He came, and left quickly and quietly.
We shared an evening and a morning together.
The time was glorious, the feelings sensational,
I glowed and his chest protruded; knowing the moment belonged to him,
> to us.

He is warm, sensuous, and his caring embrace meant to comfort, sooth,
And lift me, sent me reeling.
His touch electrified my total being.

# Love Is Like . . .

Love is like a blossoming flower
Sometimes it springs forth in full bloom
Other times it gradually and slowly
Opens in slow motion
Bringing forth its full blossom.

The flower requires the light.
Its beauty cannot be hidden
And when it reaches its full flowering
It approaches its demise
The same way it blossomed, quickly, slowly.

Love that springs forth overnight is likely to be as short-lived as its birth was quick.
Love that develops, unfolding layers of friendship, trust, closeness, loyalty, respect, and togetherness with independence, lasts forever.

# Love of a Lifetime

He is special to me and my love of a lifetime!

I love him so much that it hurts, and I don't even know how to convey it.

Isn't that something?

Can't wait to see him, and begin to miss him the moment he leaves my

Presence. I just want to be close to him.

I've never felt that way about another human being.

There need not be any words spoken, no explanations, just closeness.

Sometimes that is all I want and anything else would spoil it.

Is that special or not?

# My Loss, My World

I'll never again know the comfort and solace of his arms,
The warm soothing rays of sunshine emanating from his smile
His tender touch and the sweetness of his lips.

I can't bear the thought of losing him,
Of not being able to talk to him,
To share my heart, my hopes,
My challenges and my fears.

He'll be at home, at peace and sharing with another
But my life will never be the same.
I'll always remember, relish, and cherish those tender moments
When we looked into each other's eyes
And discovered ourselves staring back at us . . .
wanting to be together, to be one.

No mere words can begin to describe the feelings of being together,
Of being apart, of wanting to see,
To touch,
To take all of him,
To be with him.

# You Are Always There, Here in My Heart

No matter where I am, you are there.
As I sit in silence, I see your face.
In the crowded café' with music blasting and deep into conversation, you
    are there.

My favorites are playing and you are there.
I read the paper and wonder what you would say to this story;
What your response would be to that editorial.
I hear your laughter from the comics and your gut wrenching laughter at
    the comedian's monologue.

You are there when I get a sudden pain or have a splitting headache.
I get up for an Excedrin
And you hand it to me.

At the football game, you are there when the band plays.
As the crowd shouts and sways, you are there.

Sitting alone on a crowded plane going to places known and unknown,
You are there.
I feel your touch and sense your presence
You are here.

There is no place where I am that you are not.
You are always there, here in my heart.

# It

Well, it took almost two years for the patina to lose its glow;
For your interest to wane;
For you to decide, that's not what I want.

Well, maybe, as long as it stays in its' corner safe for me, hidden from view
Yet available when I need it or when I just want a private moment.

I can call on it for stimulation—mental, physical and emotional.
Then back to its box stored somewhere in a dark corner until I'm ready
    again.

Out it will come but not too far, not so others will see or know.
Even when there is a legitimate reason, a professional reason,
It must stay hidden. No one must know.

I simply want to use the talent, seek and get advice,
Think through and formulate ideas with it.
Use it to reflect and shape my own ideas;
Get the best it has to offer without acknowledging it.

I don't really love it. It is convenient, available,
Pliable, flexible and mostly non-resistant.
It is available at my beck and call.
It is mine but I'm tired of it.
How do I put it back? Give it back, forget it?

# The Dilemma of Moonlight Love

At times, like trying to leave, remember?
She's already missing him and she
can't stand it. Although she loves him beyond
question, it is difficult to
realize that he is in a world of which she can never
be a part. Although he may be
sitting next to her, she can't reach out and touch him,
nor he her. They will never
experience the glow of the sun; only the dimness of
moonlight. To know
unconditionally that she will always be in the shadows,
and the narrow confines of a
forbidden garden, steels her resolve while breaking
her spirit. Perhaps distance,
and time, will begin to reveal and unravel the veil
shielding the light. Perhaps
the way will then be clearer. What a dilemma!

# Priorities

I love him more than life itself,
But I'm not what he needs.
And if I am true to myself, he's not what I need.
The blanket of pain that covers me every time he has to take care of his priorities,
Sets my heart on fire,
Floods my eyes with tears,
And renders electric shocks to my system.

He truly has his priorities in order.
I don't, I look to him and set everything around him,
He sets everything around others,
They are his priorities.
I am as "catch can."

# The Lonely Trek

What do I do when I'm lonely? Where do I go? Can I hold your hand and walk with you? The road narrows as we walk, and the pavement runs out. We walk down a grassy slightly-worn path it seems for hours. Then I notice that the grass fades and there is sand. The sand becomes whiter and whiter, and in the distance I see water. As we get closer, I can see the ripples, crabs crawling on the shore, small holes in the sand sucking inward, something jumping out of the water! It is big, and I only glimpse it at first from the corner of my eye. It startles me, and I watch for it to jump again. It doesn't jump, but I see a shadow of a monster floating just beneath the surface, and suddenly it rises above the water, sleek, shiny, molded, black-gray glass as graceful as a trained ballerina. It seems suspended in air, and just as suddenly, with a gracious dive that can't be duplicated, it is gone. I wait to see it again, and moments later somewhere in the distance merging with the sky I see it, that graceful, beautiful figure teasing the limits of the air and earth and the depth of the ocean, merging air, water, and earth.

I sit there beside you enfolded in my memory, our arms entwined, talking, basking in the sun, enjoying the fall breeze, as the water ripples, and the waves swell, rush in, and sweep out again and again. The salty air gathers in your nostrils and fills your lungs with desire, desire for life, for love, for me. We play the game and retreat to our world again, alone, together, separate, as one, and never to be parted.

And then I awaken and you're not there. I am alone again with my memories, my heart pounding, my breathing unsteady, and my head wondering, where did he go?

# The Question Is

The question is, can I imagine life without you? As I struggle with my doubts and fears, with our differences, I am confused, and saddened by my perceptions of our possibilities.

Though I like being alone, I'm not a loner—you are.

I occasionally enjoy social groups. I don't think you do.

I love traveling, going to new and different places, going to old familiar haunts, taking short trips as an energy outlet for relaxation and renewal; you don't.

You seem to have dug your trench in the hard red clay, and refuse to budge, or to even discuss it.

You have this enduring and intense trait of being able to compartmentalize, and weed out everything but your priorities.
And nothing or nobody will be allowed to interfere—they would be unwanted intrusions.

Emotions, when they are evident, are in their boxes too and removed only when it's the proper time and place, when you have deemed them so, when you decide to release them. And then you pack them away again for another appropriate occasion.

I remember, I haven't forgotten, and I don't want to repeat those times. But even so, for me at least there has always been more than a professional and business focus.
Sometimes the boxes fall from the shelves and from their compartments in untidy tumbles, scrambling their contents mixed with fierce emotions—
sadness and joy
pain and healing
love and its denial
wanting and giving

Sometimes I just want the elusive you:
Unclothed, unarmed, bare and naked, stripped of your defenses and your compartments, timeless and ageless, spontaneous, unplanned, "spur of the moment" you.

What saddens me is that I know deep in the recesses of my heart that this will never be.

# Transformation

I sit lonely, daydreaming, and wondering and then the phone rings.
His sultry voice is on the other end.
My heart skips a beat and then stops beating momentarily.
Hearing him . . . life begins anew
Each time I hear his voice, see his face, and feel his touch.

Life will never be the same . . .
I've felt the depth, the delight, the ecstasy of his
Extraordinary love and he has transformed me and my world.

# Friendship

# Merry Christmas 2007

To a Friend,

At this time of year, we are reminded of the goodness of mankind and the tremendous potential for that goodness to bring peace and to make the world a better place to live for those who suffer in illness, are without food, shelter, clothing and the basic securities that so many of us take for granted.

We pause to share our love with family and friends and to give special thanks for our bountiful blessings. In a festive atmosphere we feast on the best delicacies and drink the smooth drinks of our choice. We laugh, play and in so many ways use this special time to say to those we care about that we love them and we lift them up.

The Christmas season is my favorite time of the year. It is the happiest and most joyful time and yet the saddest for me. Because I love the season so much, I want to share it with all who are special to me. Most of those closest to me will be here at home this year while others can only be reached in the depths of my heart. I pray for their safekeeping, good health and the strength that only love can provide. This Christmas, 2007, is truly special for me. I am thankful for my recovery from cancer and my health. But I am saddened by the absence of that special someone—you.

May you bask in the glow of family and friends and may you be embraced by love!

May the memories of love, hearth and home warm your heart, strengthen you and sustain you through the years to come.

PS
I have included a little box of goodies. I hope just going through the box brings you joy and happiness as is intended. Take the time to savor each gift and remember!

Merry Christmas, and may you have many, many more!

Love,
Altha

# Happy Father's Day

Friday, June 13, 2008

Friend,

Thanks for restoring my faith, securing my trust, and uplifting my spirits especially when I needed these the most. You even have me sitting in church many Sundays!

Even though you are not a biological father, you are indeed a father to many. I notice your caring and fatherly support of your protégés, those you informally adopt, and your staff and many friends. So many depend on you, but you love your role in their lives, and their adulation. There are probably many others of whom you are not aware, whose lives you have touched, and who idolize you.

Have a Happy Father's Day and be reminded that you are special to me and many others.

I hope that you enjoy the flowers and when you get tired of them indoors, replant them outdoors. The Florida Trend magazine is a way of keeping up with the business going-on and environment in Florida. The brochure is probably the best descriptive information I could get on the area where Doby Lee's Houseboat is. In fact, in the picture with them all lined up, hers is probably the fourth or fifth from the right end. You indicated that you would like to come down to recuperate, relax and fish, so this is it! We look forward to your coming and it's all yours! Everybody else will be working during the week so you can truly relax and have some fun. Everything is there. It is just a house on the water.

So, as I note on your subscription gift, . . . "For all the young and old you counsel, advise and support, you are a father."

Altha

# Happy New Year!

To a Friend,

I hope that you have had a very restful, recreational, and giving holiday. May 2003 bring you the blessings you so richly deserve, and the opportunity to continue to pursue your dreams. May you begin and end the year trying never to have to say, "I'm sorry," but if it is appropriate, hasten to do so. When I think of the past year, I cannot help but reflect on meeting, working with and getting to know my new found friend. The song "From a Distance" is very appropriate to my thoughts now. I could not have known the depth of your spirit, the beat of your very own drum, and your profound intellect, until I got closer. Nor would I have known the brightness with which your soul shines through your smile, your intense belief in the goodness of man and God's salvation without talking to you, querying you, and yes, sometimes even challenging you. Never, have I known you to be without faith and a deep abiding love for mankind, especially those less fortunate, and your God.

Yes, you deserve the riches in stow for you. May you and yours enjoy, share and recreate the Lord's bounty. Have a very Happy New Year's Day and may happiness dominate all of the days that follow!

# Missing My Friend

I cannot begin to say how much, how often, how deeply, and how sincerely I miss my friend.

There is no description for it.

Only the look in my eyes, the tautness of my skin, the wrinkle of my brow, and the hole in my heart can tell the time, the condition, and the story of my loss.

I miss the secrets shared, the impromptu conversations about almost anything, the hearty laughs, the words of encouragement, and the provocative discussions where we disagreed on political, social, and religious issues, but forgot about the disagreement while thinking of the other's point of view.

It was a storied friendship.

I have never had another like it.

We admired each other but were just friends.

We looked to each other for solace, for bounce backs, for encouragement to brush ourselves off and get up and try again, for moving ahead in spite of the disarray around us and the storms engulfing us, as well as the challenges we were facing . . . .

We had each other to look to for comfort, a safe place, and shoulder to lean on.

I miss my friend.

# My Friend, the Great Leader

Through your travels and various opportunities, you have learned lessons, and gained skills that few people will even have thought of. Your journey has been a terrific training experience. I also know that you will put it to work for the betterment of your organization, and people in general. "They" ought to make you an ambassador. We need to get you a PR person so that more people and groups will know about you outside of your business circle. Your talents, skills, knowledge, temperament, attitude, and outlook could be invaluable to the citizenry of the world. Even though I know that you see your place as limited to your business and social purposes, I wish you would extend that beyond those boundaries. Well, maybe it is through your foundation, the place from which to do "it." Now, I don't know what the proverbial "it" is yet. I can think of several venues, none to which I think you would agree.

You are one of the most focused persons I have ever known. You never lose your sense of purpose. You know who you are, and where you want to go. You have your goals clearly defined and steadily move toward them. You have a great talent for inspiring and enlisting the masses to your vision and in helping them craft their own. That's an unusual gift. Your gift of imagery is phenomenal! Perhaps, this is why I like talking with you. And, while I am on the subject, you touch people's hearts. You make them feel that they are important, and that they too have the wherewithal to accomplish for themselves, to do for themselves. Then, you are a model of all that is worth their emulating. You can stand alone on an issue. That takes strength borne of intestinal fortitude not common to most. In fact, very few people have it. You have it! You recognize, acknowledge, and effectively deal with ambiguity, and still not lose your focus. You have that rare talent to cut through the facade, the uncertainties, the shady areas, and yet emerge with a direction and a solution if necessary. Through it all, you challenge people to think, to arrive at their own solutions, to solve their own problems. You also challenge processes, and the institutions in which they dwell.

Guess what? I just realized that I have been describing the qualities of a "great leader" not just a leader. Among my favorite writers on leadership are Kouzes and Posner, authors of *The Leadership Challenge*. They boil it down to five attributes: challenge the process, inspire a shared vision, enable others to act, model the way, and encourage the heart. Wow! You are the embodiment of all of these and more.

# Semba

As I watched the Lion King, I thought of you, Semba.
I see your desire to do God's work and you make me believe.
I feel your hunger for perfection, it happens, it is, you are!
I hear your heart beat for the right way and the right thing.
I witness the products of your work and I am deeply moved.

You are driven to make good things happen for the people you serve.
You always see the silver lining, even when it is hidden from view.
You build rather than destroy; you lead rather than push.
You serve with dignity and grace, you tower above the crowd.

These are heartfelt expressions about how I see you. They are incomplete but will always be. From time to time, I will add to them and if appropriate, share them with you. Take care of you so that you can take care of your family and your mission.
Just know that you have friends to lean on when needed.

# A Note from a Friend

One day, a friend walked into my office.
As I talked on the phone and responded to a computer query, he scribbled a note to me.
"I want you in my life.
I do not expect that our togetherness
Will ever subside or cease to exist."

What a beautiful thought and gesture.
Since that day, he has been a constant in my life.
I go to him for solace, for inspiration, for comfort.
We are indeed the best of friends.
That is the love we share.
No matter where I am, what I am doing, or what I am planning, even what I am thinking,
I share it with him. He always makes me think and supports me or encourages me Or questions whether I should reconsider. If the latter, I always do.

What a marvelous person to have in my life.
Everybody needs a friend like that.

# My Friends, My Village

My friends are getting older as am I.
It seems that every time I turn, someone has pneumonia,
A weak back, arthritis in the legs or hips, cancer, heart disease,
Diabetes and a string of other ailments and complications.
From time to time, I get the notice that one of them has died,
and it is time to gather to pay tribute to that friend.
I wish they could all live forever but that is not possible.

Luckily, we can all make fun of ourselves and share many laughs still. Life without them would be difficult, dull, and bleak. I count myself as truly lucky and blessed to have had so many dear trusted and true friends. What must life be like without those we can call up and share our pains, struggles, defeats, sorrows, joys, and deep laughter?

Mine come from all walks of life. Some are from my childhood, and we have generally stayed in touch or in and out of touch for our lifetimes. One, Betty, and I started first grade together. We lived on the same street for a while and played daily with each other and our little neighborhood group. Dorothy and I, have also been friends since grade school. Our fathers were great friends and she, Betty, and I, along with other childhood friends attended Sunday school and church together. Between Sunday school and church, we would go down to Economy Drug store and get snacks for eating in church. We sat in the back of the church and played games, passed notes and sneaked to eat our snacks during church services.

At church, we also went to league together, choir practice, and all of the other activities that our church had to offer. We went to all of the church youth conferences. Each summer it seems that we went to Edward Waters College for our state Sunday School Convention. Each spring some of the elders, notably Mrs. Nims, would take us to Spook Hill and Bok Tower in Polk County and Cypress Gardens. Others too spent an inordinate amount of time with and for the church and to seeing to it that all of the youth of the church had opportunities that would not otherwise be afforded. I probably can't remember all of them but I do recall Dr. Baker, Dr. Efferson,

Dr. Perry, my great Uncle Ralph Hadley, Mr. Joe Franklin, and many others. Occasionally, we went to the National Sunday School Convention.

I have vivid memories of the National Sunday School Convention in South Carolina at Allen University. We girls (Audrey, Marva, Betty, Dorothy, Pat, Velma . . .) were packed in a room and just playing around. Audrey snapped a photo of me in my underwear, near nude and threatened to show it around. I probably would have "killed" her and the others if I hadn't gotten that negative and exposed it. That was my clue to be careful from then on. Boy, am I glad that the Internet and "My Space' and "Facebook" didn't exist then. You see, the church, the Great Bethel AME was at the heart of my development and a strong influence on my sense of self and others.

Even though I couldn't sing, Mrs. Althea Roberts, the music teacher and choir director at both Lincoln High School and Bethel AME Church allowed and encouraged me to be in both choirs. She was a wonderful teacher and even got me to the point where I could carry a tune. It's hard to believe that she like most of the other teachers at that school and church spent so much time with and for the students in extra and co-curricular activities. She developed very creative productions and concerts until they were perfected. We participated in regional and state competitions and frequently won. All of this without a salary supplement at school and no pay at church; just their professional integrity and individual need to be the best and bring out the best in their students.

Growing up and becoming me would not have been the same without what some now call mentors. I didn't see them that way because mostly they were my idols and folk who seemed to care about me. My great Aunt Lucy and Uncle Fred were key influences during my growing up. Aunt Lucy took me under her wings and taught me a lot of worldly things I wouldn't have known, like tea time with her and mint juleps. She would have me set the table and the two of us would sit and have tea with the fancy English sandwiches. I did odd jobs mostly dusting her many shelves of "whatnots" for her for which I received token pay. Aunt Lucy would give me a small amount but Uncle Fred would slip and give me more. Cousin Irie Mae Clark Woods also let me help her with household tasks, but she too would hold adult discussions with me. Even though I liked the idea of making some money, it was the encouragement and real life advice and support by them that captured my heart. Dear Aunt Pearl treated me and sometimes my siblings to real fancy parties and homemade cookies and cake with homemade ice cream. Throughout my growing-up years and even as an adult, my mom's childhood friend whom I called Aunt Naomi and her husband, Uncle Joe simply welcomed me into their home and made me comfortable. They were always interested in what I was doing and gave advice and encouraged me. I knew that they cared for me and cared deeply and that their home was my home.

Sometimes those who apparently cared for me demonstrated that caring in the form of reprimands, which I spurned. Other times it was open demonstrations of caring. Again, Augusta and Frank Nims top the list along with Josie Speed, Juanita and Miller Johnson, Sweet Pea and Matthew Estaras, Charlie and Ruth Jenkins, and my great aunt Lucy. There were also Edna and Zeora Hersey, Lessie Sanford, Emma Fields, Ruby Holmes, Acquilina Howell, Pilar Rhaney, Mildred Cooper, my great aunt Pearl, FlorazelleTeele, Eunice Carter, and Christine Knowles, and several more. The latter two whom I considered mean at the time were forceful and relentless that I toe the line. Even though they were good friends of MaDear's and taught at the same school, they took it upon themselves to see that I was diligent in getting my work done to the very best of my ability and that I didn't do any shoddy work or anything beneath what they thought I could produce. Christine would send me to the office for any minor thing and insist that I not come back until I buckled down to do a better job than I had. She taught business courses and especially typing in which I had very little interest. But thank God, she insisted that I learn to type.

Mrs. Carter was famous for her study guides. She would give them to her classes to guide them in their study of civics and government. The questions on the guides were reconfigured to ask questions in class and one had better be prepared daily to answer and defend your answer. She also gave frequent written tests that required mostly essay responses. I generally made "As" on her tests and for the end of the grading period. However, immediately following one grading period, but before the grades were officially issued via report cards, she asked me a direct question to which I gave the correct response but faltered in my defense. She reprimanded me for not being prepared and told me that even though I had received an A for the last grading period she was changing my grade because her

"A" students were always prepared. Was I mad! But no amount of pleading even by the principal and my parents could make her change my grade from a B back to an A. Rather than make a US Supreme Court case of it I accepted the grade. In fact, I believe that Eunice Carter would have gone to jail before she changed that grade.

Josie Speed, the notorious English teacher whose classes most tried to avoid, was also a perfectionist. I think she taught me English every year in junior and senior high school except for tenth grade when Evangeline White Tolliver taught literature. She was the youngest teacher at the school and also an outstanding teacher. In seventh through ninth grades, the emphasis was on grammar, sentence structure, and composition basics. Most importantly, we had to diagram sentences. I hated diagramming even though I was good at it. I expressed in class one day that "It is a waste of time to diagram sentences over and over again." Mrs. Speed immediately responded with something like, "You will know how to write and speak English perfectly for having done this!" Of course, I didn't believe her. But she was right! She was also the sponsor for the school's newspaper and for students selected to write for the local paper, *The Tallahassee Democrat*. I was one of the student writers for both papers and because of her and my father, did well in composition and literature class in college. That background served to further advance my writing skills.

I attended college in my hometown but spent two years on or near campus. Consequently, most people on campus knew me. Mrs. Cooper, assistant dean of women, guided me throughout my freshman year. Mrs. Kidd encouraged me and insisted that I could conquer the higher math courses that she taught. During my year in Diamond Hall, Mrs. Teele, Mrs. Littles, and Mrs. Petties, watched over me like hawks. Once an older young man, a naval officer, came to visit me and Mrs. Teele told him that he was too old for me and not to come back. I later teased her that she ran my future husband away. He was only seven years older and later became a very successful professional and businessman.

These folk helped to shape me and to strengthen the values my parents instilled at home. Every kid should be so lucky as to have several adults to guide and look after them in conjunction with the values their parents instilled. They were my village caretakers.

In later life, it was those who seemed to embrace me and later, George and Russell took us in and under the protection of their friendship and by association had others to embrace us. For all of them, I am grateful. What would it have been like to move to a town not knowing anybody and finding our way? The Brock's in Ocala took me as their daughter and big sister to their children, Gloria and Daryl. The Hamptons also of Ocala encouraged my efforts to see the world and allowed their son, Kerry to go on a six-week study tour of Denmark and Europe with me. They also influenced Lottie Donaldson to send her son, Walter.

On to Miami and then to Durham with my husband and the protective armor offered by Frank and Vea Bright and their young children Kenneth and Karen. Oh, how I loved them. They introduced me and my hubby to Durham. Also welcoming us with open arms were my hubby's friends, Juanita and Sonny, Skeepie and Clara, Robert and Clara, Carolyn and Bert, Carroll and Bernice, Carolyn and George and a whole host of others. With their association and influence we were accepted and invited to most of the social functions of Durham.

After George completed law school, we moved to High Point. Even though I went to graduate school in Chicago, High Point became home. We lived there for five years and our son, Russell was born there. There is no way to describe the friendship of Barbara and Otis Tillman, Marlene and Sam Chess, Sally and Bob Brown, Loretta and Bill Marshall, Meg and Perry Little and Al and Hattie Campbell. They took us into the bosom of their homes and ensconced us in their worlds. It was a glorious time of joyful and rewarding experiences. In fact, the Tillmans' became our son's godparents.

Another move introduced us to the Daytona Beach area and friends with whom we are still connected even though death has taken its toll on some of them. Life would have been less comfortable and exciting without Emmie and John Frink, Morris and Rose Carter, Alma and Lonnie Brown, Alba and Sam Berry as well as Larry and Paul Hyde and Josephine. Again, we were wrapped in the comfort of friendships that introduced us to the social world of Daytona. There was never a dull or an idle moment unless we sought it. We entertained together and were entertained by them. All of our children were like cousins—Bruce and Jacque Frink; Loneen, LT, and Alan Brown; Dorian Carter and Susan Hyde. All of the kids among the families as with those in Durham and Highpoint (Quita, Bonnie, Tammie, and Chip Tillman; and Eva and Janet Chess) and now Daytona, referred to the adults as aunt and uncle. If you didn't feel like cooking, you could always call and see who had a dish in the oven or a pot on the stove. Once discovered, we could just say, "We'll be right over." Or get someone to go out to dinner with us.

Tallahassee became our last home and it was full circle for me. It was the city in which I grew up. I had not wanted to ever move back home but my husband took a position there encouraged by Da'Doby. We were able to reconnect with some old friends but mostly to connect with many new folk as well. It is also where my husband lived his last days. Even so, the years in Tallahassee held many fond memories and like for other things some sad and hurtful ones as well. That's life! There is both pain and pleasure.

# This Christmas, 2001

To a friend

I don't think that this is an effect of 9/11, but the growing realization that I don't want things anymore. Of course, I have plenty of them already. But I have reached the point in life that the "things" don't matter. Now, I appreciate gifts perhaps more than anybody because of who is giving them and the thought behind them. Gifts to me need not be expensive, the most fashionable or the day's most sought after fad. They simply need to come from the heart. However, a note, a phone call or card is always appreciated.

In an effort to get all of my things in order for Xmas, I stopped by the cleaners to pick up my clothing. Mike, the very pleasant young man, who works there, asked if I was going to get everything I wanted for Xmas. I was somehow surprised as I responded that I didn't want anything except health, happiness, love, and peace. I suppose what I meant was that I didn't particularly crave material things or anything that money could buy. Probably, I have been developing to this point for some time but the focus has recently crystallized. Certainly, I didn't want anything last year either, but my perspective was clouded from my loss of George, and all I would have wanted was to have him back whole.

You know, sometimes it takes a whole lot of living to realize what is important in life. Lucky is the man, woman, or child who can reach this milestone early. Mostly, it takes time to bruise and learn to heal and to see them as minor bumps along life's way. It takes time to love, really love in friendship, familially and love that exist between a man and a woman who have gotten to know, encourage, support, and trust each other. And it takes time to believe and see life as simple because you are able to strip away all of the hurts, frills, and fancies and go to the core, to look beyond the curves and detours in the road and see our destination as the journey it is.

Can we short circuit all of this? Should we? Perhaps, but we will miss some very important lessons if we do. Lessons of survival, endurance, responsibility, commitment, resilience, love, appreciation of things natural, simple and small, persistence; lessons learned in that nonnegotiable medium of time—time which does not stand still and time that moves forward whether you are counting or not. Thus, once we have the lessons and have barely learned them, we look back and attempt to grasp the past to reveal our epiphany—to share and apply our wisdom. But our feet are firmly planted in the fleeting present time and not too distant future.

As I revel in this my sixty-second Christmas, I think of my myriad experiences and opportunities for growth and development. I'm grateful to my teachers, my grandfather, my father and mother, siblings, cousins, friends and enemies alike, mentors, circumstances, children, my surrogate mothers and fathers, and especially my young friends. I learned from each of them. Some were formally educated, others weren't, but I learned from them and the circumstances as well. I learned and actually mastered many of those lessons, leaving no pages unread and few experiments untested. But there were some lessons that I did not even attempt. I suppose I have to stick around to learn some of those.

Well, I didn't mean to get philosophical on you on this glorious morn. You are truly blessed. You have a loving and warm family. Cherish and love them as I know you do. Never take them for granted. This is a special time to show that love and appreciation. I can't remember who said it, but it goes, "You can give without loving, but you can't love without giving." Give them that special gift that only you can, YOU.

MERRY CHRISTMAS! My best regards to the family.

# You Were Just Here and *Poof*, You're Gone

You disappeared as quickly as you had appeared those years ago. Your death was sudden and shocking. It is difficult to go on without your support, your counsel and advice, your understanding and encouragement. Although it has only been a few years, it seems like an eternity. It was with you that I cried, grieved, and opened up my soul. It was you whose shoulders were broad enough to bring me back from the abyss. And when I got back, you were there to carry me across, to show me the way and to make me look beyond despair. It was you who said, "You will be all right," but you stayed nearby to be sure and to encourage me. You didn't hold my hand but you helped me to take my first steps back to sanity.

We became soul mates; you were the living embodiment of the concept. It was so easy talking to you and you to me. I had only experienced a similar synergism with George. It wasn't sex, it wasn't romanticism it was the deepest friendship. Anything was a go and could be placed on the table for easy viewing, examination, and discussion. We didn't always agree but we easily disagreed agreeably. We seldom got angry with each other and if we did, it was short-lived. Further, the anger was always about the other looking out for her/himself.

Our topics were wide-ranging from philosophy, politics, education, religion, poetry, to jokes and the most personal feelings and relationships . . . mine, yours, and anybody else's. I could literally read your mind and you mine, anticipate your next move and you mine. You'd ask, "What are you thinking?" and then tell me what it was. Perhaps the most precious moments were those of virtual entanglement through solitude. No words were necessary, no need to break the silence or to explain. Just be, think, and begin the conversation again as if what was on our minds was laid bare. I was always amazed at those moments of revelation, epiphanies.

You were here for only a short while. I am thankful for your presence and your friendship. I valued your friendship above all others. There must have been a purpose for our meeting, our chance encounters, our sharing, and our sense of oneness. We always shared stories, our writings, and when I had good news or bad, you were the first with whom I wanted to share it. And when you were troubled or perplexed, you'd call and talk about it and I knew you felt better about the situation. Most often, it was simply listening to each other work through our problems.

We must have come across each other for a

# Loss and Grief

# Grieving

What is it that we miss when we lose a loved one?
Why do people mourn so, and for so long? Is it necessary?
I think I have some answers but not necessarily the answer.
Perhaps there is no single answer.
And, perhaps the loss is in direct proportion
to the length and intensity of the relationship.
A mere acquaintance, a distant co-worker, a casual friend,
do not generate the same depth of loss as the
loss of a child whom we loved dearly,
or the husband of thirty-plus years with whom we did everything,
Or the friend who was there at our beck and call
And with whom we shared everything.
No, the more entwined that other person is in our lives and in our hearts,
even if the entanglement is negative,
The more we will miss her or him,
And the more we will grieve.

A visit to the grocery store and a walk down the aisles
spark a memory of times forever lost and a longing for the past.
Buying one steak rather than two and generally having to downsize your shopping.
Passing his favorites, the fat wieners, and hot dog buns later to be fixed and piled high
with mustard, onions, slaw, and chili,
and the vanilla ice cream to be steeped with hot chocolate sauce,
pains the heart and glistens the eyes.
Meal time, going out to breakfast, lunch, or dinner,
which become less frequent, signal the loss.
Going to church and missing him seated next to you,
or in the acolytes corner, or the choir,
even more severely underscores the loss.
Having the other side of the bed empty and realizing
that the special person in your life will forever be absent from that
special place in your heart and your bed and home.

This absence will reverberate through your mountains and valleys many times over,
until you create another life with other memories.
Even then it does not disappear, its intensity simply weakens and its light dims,
leaving its absence less painful.

The problem is you have come to like, value, appreciate and desire the way it was.
That has become your standard, your values,
the measures by which you grade life's experiences.
For the past twenty, thirty, forty, or even all of your life,
going out alone has never been a practice.
And, perhaps without even recognizing it,
you internalized that going out meant being with that special somebody,
that you don't go out alone to the movies, to eat, to the ballgame, the club,
the concert, the banquet, to visit friends,
for a Sunday ride, or even to church.
No, going out meant being with that special person.

Perhaps, it was a friend, a brother, or a sister with whom you enjoyed
Special times together, quiet walks, special talks, dinner together, sharing secrets, discussing their and your problems, trustingly and fearlessly,
Knowing that the secrets and relationships revealed were safe in that person's heart.
Sharing a knowing glance when a remark is made,
A phone call to discuss a hot political issue and to berate the other side,
Smiling in the face of adversity but knowing that that special person feels your discomfort, shares your pain, and will provide comfort and enfold you in the safety of his arms, her bosom of trust and true friendship.

Picking up the pieces of our lives is so much easier said than done.
Because our values, our standards by which we live have been violated, "picking up the pieces and laying them straight again, becomes so much more difficult. Rather than a straight path of neatly laid stones, it becomes a roughly crafted maze. We'll have no specific solution or pattern to go by.
We'll just have to make it as we go.

Passersby, and those who have not experienced the deep and abiding losses of life, don't really understand what you are experiencing.
Some say, "Why can't she just move on?"
They haven't been there. Unfortunately, most of us can't have true empathy for a situation until we have "worn and walked in the moccasins of the Indian."
The longer we live the more likely it is that we will understand.
Therein lies the true value of experience.

Grieving is not "bad." Like the loss it represents, it is a natural process and one of life's distasteful and dreaded but necessary human experiences.
Experiences we will all have if we live.
Experiences, from which we can benefit, grow and that will strengthen us.
Not to experience loss and not to grieve is not to have lived and not to be human.
Nor is grief restricted to death. It could signal a loss through divorce,
Estrangement from a child, the ending of a friendship or the severance of a
Deep relationship with a lover.
Whatever the cause of the loss, we will grieve.
No grief, no loss!

# Holidays—Christmas and New Year's 2003

Christmas Day came and went, slowly, happily and painfully.

It was a day of joy, friendship, the big family gathering, love, and peace. But with it came a bath of sadness, of loss, and remembrance of days gone by. At no other time in my life, save the past three years (and four Christmases), have I felt so utterly alone, helpless, and without that very special friend, companion, lover, soul mate, and trusted partner.

As a child, I looked to my grandfather as the apple of my eye. Later, my father, uncles, and male cousins would share that role, followed by my first boyfriend, and one whom I thought then would be my partner for life. Actually, he was more of a true friend than a sweetheart although we were in love; we were first the best of friends. We shared our dreams and hopes, and invented the future through them.

There was almost always that special male, a soul mate, but for the past few Christmases, I was left only with my memories of unconditional love, and true friendship, with no hope of a companioned future, and my son. Oh, what a son he is! Like his father, he is compassionate, loving, kind, and caring. He is demonstrative of that affection and boldly proclaims me as not only his first love, but his number one for now and forever! Who knows what forever is.

It is my sincerest and true hope that he finds someone whom he can love with all his heart and soul and who loves him the same. If I like her that would just be gravy on the meat. He has had a great example, a model of what fatherhood and a life mate should be. If he is lucky, he too will craft a life with another that rewards him with the pain and joy of being in another's skin, of living for and with another, of being able to finish her sentences and her his, of selfless giving and receiving, of standing with another in good times and bad, and not wanting it any other way. Oh, if he is lucky, he will find that special someone and repeat the vows, "Till death do us part." And mean it with all of his heart.

This Christmas, more than any other, I have reminisced, missed, and regretted my loss. I have realized, that mine may be a life forever without a special someone to share the early morning sunrise, the evening sunset, and all the joys, satisfactions, disappointments, challenges, and conflicts in between. As I face the New Year in a few days, I embrace what is to come. I have not yet finished my life. I have made mistakes in the past and I will continue to make them, and hopefully learn from them. I have not always done my best, but my spirit remains strong, bold, and undaunted. I may head in another direction, stay the course, or modify my current course. Whatever the future brings, I look forward to shaping its course as it will shape mine and me.

# A Treasured Jewel

(Among my whispers to my husband during his terminal illness)


I can't bear the prospect of losing you.
They say that life goes on but how are we supposed to manage without you?
Do you realize that for the past thirty-four years we have talked almost daily?
A higher value is placed on anything that is rare—
A rare stone is a gem; rare paintings are treasures;
Rare coins, books, and cars are collectors' items.
And, you, my dear, are the rarest treasure of all, a jewel!
Memories of times with you will sustain us forever.

# A Journey through Loss and Grief

It has taken me nearly four years to write about something I know up close and personal. Four years! I just knew that I would be able to write that book or essay on grief because after all I had truly experienced it. But I couldn't. Every time I tried to put fingers to the keyboard to tackle the issue, my mind would go blank. I couldn't express my thoughts let alone my feelings. They seemed scrambled and frozen, never to be exposed to the sunlight. Now, I sense a gradual melting, a release. Perhaps, I am putting my pieces of the puzzle in place.

Here I am nearly four years after the death of my husband, six months later my brother for whom my husband and I were confidantes, eight months later the death of my cousin, political ally and confidante. The latter was the person whom I would call if I heard something on the radio or saw something on TV related to politics that was, "Can you believe he said that when he is doing this?" "Did you see her put him in his place?" "OK, what do we do now? They won't believe we are ready for them. Let's go get 'em." We would laugh and have some really precious moments of joy and plot, plot and plot some more. That void has not been filled either. That special, politically tainted and personal mix of closeness is rare and not likely to occur often.

My brother, Junior, was a very special person to me. When he was born, I, of course, was the oldest and adoring sister but he was also adored and doted on by my younger sister Bea. He was a beautiful baby who was very quiet and quite shy during his early years. His daughter, Kacey, reminds me so much of him. When she first went to school she never talked but I cautioned them that it did not mean that she was not aware and could not do the work. In fact, I knew she knew it and probably better than most. A similar thing happened with Junior. However, they were both soaking up all around them. Luckily, by the time Kacey came along we were more aware, appreciative and supportive of children's differences and styles.

My father, a former teacher and principal from the old school, was the supreme ruler and teacher in our house. He had no patience with differences and believed that you either knew it or you didn't. And, if you didn't you'd better get it posthaste or the belt of punishment would rain down on you. He taught us what he thought we should know as we progressed whether the teachers had gotten us there or not. Studying was not an option. We did it whether we had assignments or not and we learned to make up homework because what he would give us if we said we had none was far harder than anything the teacher could construct. Needless to say, Junior went through many sessions as a kid that caused him great pain. He didn't always get it right away not because he didn't have the smarts but because he couldn't process it normally as we had. We now know that he was dyslexic and later overcame this when our Mom took charge and got him some help. After that he soared and did better than any of us. In fact, he was brilliant!

I loved him as did all of us but we knew he was a "free agent" and would mosey in and around us as he pleased. He joined the Jehovah's Witness Church at some point in his adult life. We all kidded that he did it to keep from giving gifts on special occasions. He always hoarded his money even as a kid. While the rest of us would go out and spend our money usually on frivolous stuff, he would stash his away. When nobody else had money, Junior had money. Too bad our youngest brother Ralph would always find his hiding places and would occasionally wipe him out. Even though he wouldn't give you a gift on the occasion, he would at some time give you something, take you to dinner, lunch, or to some outing. That was his way of giving without violating his denominational beliefs.

Since my husband and I were his confidantes, he'd just appear sometimes after a long absence and sit and talk for hours. He often visited with my husband and sought his advice. He'd borrow money because he was always in a tight spot. Again, while we were spending recklessly, he was investing and buying property. But you could always bank on him paying you back. He was a man of his word. So to lose my brother six months after the death of my husband, kind'a took the wind out of my sails. Though again, I stood the test of composure and calm during and immediately after. But the toll of that loss is still fresh in my heart. I cannot get over my young brother dying and leaving his two beautiful and prized daughters, Kacey and Katrina, behind, never seeing them grow up, and never to sit by the door with his shotgun to ward off the boys as he threatened he would. I knew how much he loved those girls. He told me all the time and sought my advice on their upbringing and well-being.

My husband and I were the first ones to whom he introduced Linda, his fiancée and the first ones to whom he revealed that she was pregnant. I, in particular, along with the whole family, wore him down until he made the right decision. They were married and he treasured those girls. The greatest hurt for me in his death, was that he could no longer be with and there for them. The next most damaging and lasting impact was the unnecesssariness of his death. He had pneumonia, went to the hospital and contracted a bacterial disease in the hospital from which he died. During his comatose state which lasted for several days, we could see and feel him slipping away. I would sit by his bedside for hours and sing, "You are my sunshine, my only sunshine, you make me happy when skies are gray, you'll never know dear how much I love you, please don't take my sunshine away."

When he died my sunshine disappeared. Still today, more than four years after his death, I shed tears as I type these words reliving my loss.

My husband's death, though anticipated, left indelible marks on my soul, never to be erased or forgotten. It was he who balanced me. Like most couples who learn to "get along," we struggled and resisted changing ourselves. But in the end, we laughed about how we had both changed and met somewhere in the middle while each vacillated toward the other side from time to time carrying more weight than the other. We seemed to just "know" when the other needed our strength and we both gave without the asking and gave generously. In fact, we didn't even see it as giving, just as a natural extension of ourselves being there for and with the other person. We each took on the other as our responsibility. We just seemed to know when the other was in need and specifically what the other needed. We'd break through the walls of the Hoover Dam to do whatever needed to be done without asking and without hesitation.

So much was assumed. If he had an engagement that required my presence, even at the last minute, he knew I'd be there without question. Oh, occasionally, I'd rib him about waiting until the last minute to notify me. Likewise, I'd call him up at 6:00 p.m. and say, "Hey, we need to be at the country club at 7:00 p.m. for this reception for this person." Without question, he'd say, "I'll pick you up at 6:45 p.m." But since we both were busy professionals, we seemed to understand the stresses and strains on each other and how omissions were possible without intention of hurting.

We just understood and did what was necessary. Going to dinner and many other activities, like the movies, etc., meant going with him (and my son, when he was growing up) unless it was with a professional associate or a friend. It never meant going alone unless it was something I just wanted to do, my choice and only when I was out of town, alone.

His demise means always going alone or having to find someone to go with me. What a turn of events! Remember, my value has been shaped by now to mean, "You don't go it alone." So, now I have to really think hard and unlearn all that I have learned and valued all of my life. I also grew up in a very traditional family. My father never allowed us girls to go out alone. In the pre-teen years it was with another young adult, later with a few carefully selected girlfriends and after courtship began it had to always be with the approved young man or a group of approved friends. Going anywhere other than school or maybe church alone was not an option. Even so, being the oldest of six children, I was seldom alone except when I sought solace in the late night and early morning to do my studying in the quiet that was not possible when everyone was awake. Perhaps that is why I value privacy and the aloneness of choice now (different from going out).

And, what about being able to turn to that other self and ask, "What about this?" Can the proverbial we do this? Now, there is no one to turn to, no one to think out loud with and no one to share life's vagaries, its mountains and valleys as well as its plains. It is aloneness by force on a being taught to be together with and who values a special someone. Finding my way out this conundrum has not been easy. On the surface, to some I have made leaps and bounds without looking back. Others occasionally see the tear-stained eyes, the tear that just won't stay in the eye but gently rolls down the cheek in slow motion. Perhaps the most telling sign has been the refusal to go on a date or go by myself to balls, parties, the movies, etc. It's a slow process. I don't know if I will ever get to that unknown place of Being comfortable without a special other.

At first, I didn't grieve like I had expected to. I didn't cry at the funeral. It was all too new. I have always had perfect composure under stress and have managed my feelings well. And in fact, didn't feel the stuff I thought I would and what I suppose is expected. I guess I just react differently in my own time and space. Now, as time erodes the layers of life, I have come face-to-face with myself and my losses. It is in the quiet of the bedroom, the paying of bills and reconciliation of finances, the preparation of taxes, the consideration of property issues, consideration of investments, major purchases and selling, wanting to share the beauty of a rose, sleeping late on a Saturday morning, enjoying a bubble bath together, making a decision about home repairs, buying a car, going to the movie, selecting a household accessory, reading the paper in the family room while looking at TV and wanting to discuss the story on TV or the article in the paper, and so many other everyday experiences that sometimes bring me to the painful brink of knowing, missing, and finally acknowledging that I am alone but must go on.

I finally realized at some point along the way that memories are the only treasures we will have in later life. I know that my husband, my brother and my cousin, had some very good memories to sustain them in their darkest and fading hours. They knew they were and are loved, treasured and an essential part of my life and the family's. They too could recall in those last weeks, days, hours the glory of love and the immortality of our memories of life together. I am happy that I am able to write about this, my grief. I hope I have touched on some of what you experienced and that it helped you to remember, to glimpse back, and to see forward. Your stories will be different but relive them and treasure them.

Recently my mother died but the experience of that death is still too raw for me to deal with at this point. Perhaps later I can face the reality and pain of her death.

# Spirituality

# Thanksgiving 2001

As I reflect on this day of Thanksgiving, I realize that I have so very much for which to be thankful. Not only do I have the basic needs of food, shelter, clothing, safety, security, etc, I have them in abundance. Although I make it a point to stay grounded, stay in touch with some who are not as fortunate, I feel that I have strayed lately from tangibly helping those less fortunate except with checkbook giving. I never want to be above and beyond in my view of my worth versus that of others.

Like those of us who count our blessings through the heart, I feel blessed to have so many good friends and to enjoy the company of those like yourself whose caring support, encouragement and intellectual and creative talents are shared so bountifully with me and others. Early this morning before I went to bed, I began to reflect on my many blessings and tried to craft this note. Of course prominent among them were you and my family. However, sleep captured my body and forced me to bed before I could finish.

Although at times I feel that I can scale Mount Everest, my knees get weak when I hear the voices of loved ones, the demands of a child, the shrill of a mockingbird, see the beauty of the rose, watch the grace of the doe and all of God's grand design here on earth. His mountains green with grass, snowcapped barren and dry captivate me. The rolling brook, the tranquil lakes, the ferocious sea mesmerize me.

I wonder in amazement at his sculpture, the earth, and the whole universe. Wow! It is breathtaking. Can't you just see it in all its beauty? I am flying high above the fray. And from my position, I can see, appreciate and relish the impeccable beauty. As I get closer I begin to see the brown patches in the grass, the wilted flowers, the ant hills, and yes, the weak, the sick, the aged, and the helpless. This reminds me of the Bette Midler song, "From a Distance."

So it is with us. From a distance we only see beauty and perfection. As we get closer we see the faults, the scars, the sadness and the many struggles. But isn't it just beautiful when you can love that person or your family anyway? That is true love, true appreciation for the machine called us.

I am saddened by the plight of so many who are truly less fortunate. They scrounge the trash cans for food. They have no one to smile at them, to cuddle them, to believe in them and to lift them up and give them hope. How tragic that must be! Is that what is intended? Are they there as reminders of how things can be? Have they done something to cause their conditions? Why? Certainly the little children don't deserve the neglect, abuse, hunger, sleepless nights, and bleak futures facing them. Someone once asked me what I'd do if I won millions? I'd truly give it away to help those less fortunate to help themselves.

On this day, I thank you for being my friend. You will never know the heartfelt joy, peace and serenity you inspire. Your presence, your voice, you seem to say, "It's all right." And it is.

# Church

Sometimes while sitting in church, I often ask, "Why am I here?" although most of my life I have participated in organized religion with periods of detachment. Since my young adulthood, I have not always found it to be a meaningful spiritual experience.

So as I look around, gaze upon the crucifix, affix my eyes on the priest, choir, acolytes, lay Eucharistic ministers, the organist, and all the elements representing our denominational faith, the Episcopal Church, I reminisce about my spiritual journey.

Among my most vivid memories are those at Tanner Chapel AME Church in Palmetto, Florida, as a young child attending with my granddaddy. After moving to Tallahassee at six years of age, I encountered what would become one of the cornerstones of my life, Bethel AME Church in Tallahassee. Then, church was very meaningful, and was at the heart of my upbringing.

Although I grew up in the African Methodist Episcopal Church (AME) I occasionally visited the Methodist Episcopal Church or now the United Methodist Church. On a few occasions, I also visited my family's Church, Bethel Missionary to hear the Rev. C.K. Steele preach. He was a dynamic preacher whose messages were meaningful, inspirational and heartfelt. He and Mrs. Steele were always very warm and welcoming and she and my Mom were good friends. During my college years, I attempted to change my membership to the Episcopal Church because of its activities and attractions for college students and Fr. Brooks' inspirational leadership. However, my Mom insisted that I stay with the AME church. But because, I, like so many others, was disappointed in the minister at my home church at the time, I stopped going to church there.

The pastor at Bethel during most of my growing up years was Rev. H. McNeil Harris. He and his wife, Mama Harris, had no children of their own but loved the youth of the church and supported enrichment efforts for our development. They turned the basement of the church into a recreation area for youth. And, whenever we had choir, drama or other rehearsals or activities at the church, Mama Harris would have a tray of good ole homemade cookies for us.

Today, I am reminded why I still attend church, and it has little to do with the service except that sometimes we do have "good" music and some meaningful sermons. No matter, any church service and its teachings remind us that there are grand rules in life and that there is a divine whose teachings we are to follow. Church helps to imprint these teachings in the very core of our being and reinforces them each and every service. The teachings help us to see beyond ourselves and to see ourselves as a part of and connected to humankind and a higher order.

Church is also one of the few tight-knit places where we can observe as well as experience the entire breadth of human life. This is particularly true in my congregation and other small ones. We witness the pregnancy, see and observe the newborn baby, watch it grow into an active and restless toddler, develop into a young child, a pre-teen, a teenager, a young adult, and an adult. Most of the children, teens and young adults in my church will serve in some capacity on the altar or as an altar boy or girl. If one is fortunate enough, one can witness the evolution of that baby growing and developing as a young adult, marrying, and having children of their own who repeat the same march through time. Isn't it wonderful?

The young couples, middle-aged adults, our seniors, and those close to demise all exist within the parameters of our churches. And my church is small enough to get to know all members and be with all of them. Every Sunday following church, there is a fellowship in the church's Parish Hall either with a full meal or heavy hors d'oeuvres. The observation of the circle of life and the opportunity to fellowship make for a very rewarding experience!

Epilogue

*Note*: I recently attended Bethel Missionary Baptist Church and was truly inspired by the minister's message. The Reverend, Dr. R. B. Holmes delivered a dynamic and inspirational sermon—*Choose Life: The Joy of Making the Right Choice, that* appeared to be aimed at the youth of the church, but the message is applicable to adults alike. It reminded me of the sermons Rev. Steele used to deliver. There were messages inherent in the sermon that all could walk away with and that could be used to guide us in our daily lives.

# Thanksgiving

I am in awe of God's handiwork! Sometime during the early morning hours, I was awakened by my storm alert system . . . . I tried to ignore it except the trying kept me awake. Later this morning I heard the patter of rain from my open bathroom window. Now, after a near sleepless night, I sit at my computer to capture my reflections of praise and thanks and to highlight some of the many ways in which God's work is manifested and omnipresent in our lives. It is not always evident to some of us that he is at the helm in some situations or at least we don't always think of it in that manner.

As I gaze from my desk, I witness again the beauty of our world. My tall pine trees are swaying to the rhythm of the wind. The lower trees and bushes sway too. The haze of a fine mist left from the rain frames and penetrates the scenery. Raindrops linger on the dying crepe myrtles, gardenias and assorted shrubbery. The majestic camellias in all their glory stand alone in full bloom as fall fades into winter. Ginger plants bearing their last blooms frame the front flower bed. The summer drought weakened some camellias and other fall and winter bearing plants so their blooms won't appear this year.

It's funny how some plants of the same species will bloom no matter what the situation while others wilt and dwarf in their glow. It reminds me of us humans. Some are resilient, persistent and find ways to grow, thrive and become their personal best. They just never give up!

What is it that makes some plants of the same species, planted in the same flower bed at the same time thrive while others' growth is thwarted? Is it that they are different within from the start; a difference that we can't see? Does it take more fertilizer, light or water or less for some? Likewise, why is the human response to similar or the same environmental stimuli different? We are different and we respond differently to the variety of stimuli presented by the world.

This brings me to the reason for this great day which gives us an opportunity to "*stop,*" get off the fast track, commune and reunite with family and friends and to reflect on the many blessings we enjoy. Many of us have had challenges which we may have initially seen as curses or just bad luck. Most of us will overcome those challenges, solve the inherent problems and emerge stronger than ever before for without these our ability to survive in the world is weakened. All of us have had a bounty of blessings; the rain to wash away the dust and dirt, the sunshine to dry up the rain and to brighten our days, the flowers, birds and all of God's creatures each with its own mission to observe in wonder and the trees to shade us and sometimes protect us.

Some of us are more fortunate than others and no matter what our station in life, it is clear that we are dependent on each other. I believe that our mission in life is to not only help ourselves and to enrich our own lives but to reach out and help those less fortunate. They are all around us but sometimes we don't see or feel them.

Today, I took about twelve cakes, cartons of cookies and lots of pies to Project Annie, a local holiday feeding program, to help feed those who may not have a Thanksgiving meal otherwise and provided a check for staples. That is easy. What would have been more helpful would have been to cook, serve, clean up and greet those for whom the dinner is prepared. Even more important, would have been the task of helping them to find or create jobs so that they could provide for themselves, providing resources for training, helping them to secure adequate shelter and clothing for them and their families would lift them beyond the single day dinner to a level of self sufficiency. Unfortunately, this year I was not physically able to do much more. Hopefully, in years to come I will resume the real task of helping others to help themselves.

# I Care About . . .

I always appreciate my friends' special concerns for me. As a result of my cancer diagnosis, surgery, and the subsequent healing process, a friend, Janie, asked to come and pray with me. This friend's prayer was special and caused me to reflect . . .

I say to my friend, you have brought me more to the center, wherever that is. I don't think you realize how spiritual I really am. I am perhaps not like most people in expression of it. I prefer to live it, be it. I think my spirituality is caring and caring deeply for others, being concerned about their welfare on a day-to-day basis, and acting in a quiet way to do what I can for those less fortunate.

I care about the loss of trees, and the green coverage of the earth; about the function and beauty of flora and fauna; about their and humans beauty, and the bountiful ways that beauty is manifested; about how we live, and how we can live in harmony with nature but don't; and I care about our condition, love, and the absence of it, wealth and poverty, and how we use or misuse our gifts; how we treat each other; about life, living, loss, grieving and recovery, and the resulting metamorphosis; and how we seem to forget that everything and everybody are parts of a grand system that works in sync with every other part.

I care about maintaining those structures like family, church, government, and others that are changing us and the world around us. I care that when this ever-changing world has finally reached its infinite state of being—an ever-changing one, that we will have what we can be happy with. But I care because I know that some of us are uncomfortable with the evolution, its rapid pace, and never ending movement.

We are born, we live, we rejoice, we mourn, we contemplate, we act, we love, we hate, we fight, we struggle, and we die, all to the omnipotent, omnipresent rhythm of life and death. The beat goes on; it's steady and ever changing . . . .

# Travel

# Zanzibar

Just the sound of the name, Zanzibar, conjures up images of exotica, magic. I felt as if I had stepped back in time as I wound my way through the narrow alleys that led to Arabian, European, African, and Asian dwellings and businesses alike. They stood side by side as did the mosque, temple, and parish church. These symbols of distant, dissimilar cultures resonate throughout the city in its people, food, dress, languages, art, sounds, and even its architecture.

For example, the door was a noticeable architectural feature. These huge, ornately carved edifices stood as a testament to the country's cultural heritage. They appeared the same or at least so similar as to defy differences. But upon closer inspection, the arched doors versus the square inlays and spikes signified either Indian or Arabian culture.

Strolling along the alleyways and streets, I encountered the scents of spices, the roar of the sea, the Muslims "call to prayer," the days catch, and the aromas of the island's exotic flowers wafting through the air at times as separate scents and sound that later converged and emerged as one. Walking through downtown, the magic continues as I observed shops of all kinds with native art, modern art, and designer clothing as well as dress unique to the island, restaurants and cafés, luxury hotels with five-star services and décor of the finest and most delicate silks and other fabrics, jewels and jewelry that tease the eyes.

Just a stone's throw from the central downtown area was the central market that echoed both the ancient and the modern. It was a mixed open-air market that showcases all of Zanzibar—products of spice farms, samples of fresh coconut juice, teas, and meat, one could lounge on the beach, float through art galleries of native art, or you could just be and choose the familiar. Here visitors could buy the very latest electronics, clothing reflective of all ages and styles, ancient coins, spices and teas for which the island is known and everything the sea has to offer. This broad array of Zanzibar's offerings at once appeared to stand still in time and to glide freely among the ages and through time.

As I walked down an aisle just near and facing the ocean, I spotted men kneeling on the floor but could not discern what they were doing or what they were doing it to. Only after I got right up on it could I determine that they were beating something large with large rocks. The "thing" that was foreign to me upon which they were beating on the naked, dirty, cement floor which people had walked on earlier was a large octopus! Yuk! Needless to say, I was nearly sick to my stomach. That octopus appeared larger than the men beating on it, and I'm told they were tenderizing it. "No more calamari for me," I said. That statement in a city known for its delicacies of the sea was almost nonsensical.

After tiring of the walking and feasting both my eyes and palate on everything representative of Zanzibar, it was time to sit and reflect on the day's adventures. So I and my friends boarded a bus to the Spice Island farms to sample the freshly grown and highly marketed spices of the island. The trip there was well worth the ride. We could see even more of how the people lived, the farms, the workers, the ocean, and some of its waterfront properties and beaches. As we neared the farm we selected to visit, the scent of the spices was almost overwhelming. Nutmeg, cinnamon, sapphron, tumeric, and the vast array of other spices and teas tickled our senses and tricked our appetites into tasting everything and buying an abundance of what most of us would never use back home because most don't cook.

We were spent after an hour or more and boarded the jitney back to our hotel. I could barely make it back to my room with all of my packages while wondering who had enough space in her suitcase to carry some of my load back home. After a soothing shower and just sitting for a few moments to relax, I was hungry and called my friends to see if they were ready for dinner. Everyone agreed that we should try to beat the crowd. The concierge recommended a restaurant on the beach with an open-air porch.

We took his advice and walked to the restaurant. We chose seating overlooking the beach where again we could see the dhow boats coming in from the day's sea hunting and in the near distance, unloading some of their catch. Families and tourists were playing on the beach, swimming and taking advantage of the fine white sandy beach's offerings. After a short while, the waiter came to take our appetizer and drink orders. I ordered calamari! After I had tasted the thin and crisply fried rings dipped in a peculiar but tasty sauce, everybody laughed and I suddenly realized I had already broken my pledge that I would not eat calamari again. I swear it was the best I have ever had. They attempted to placate me by saying, "It's not octopus, and they are not handled the same." Right! No matter I had already taken the plunge and loved it.

This island off the coast of mainland Tanzania is a bed of lush greenery, sandy beaches, offshore waters filled with the dhow fishing boats steered by triangular cloth sails and the smell of spices and seafood so common to the area. From a visitor's perspective, acculturation is not immediately evident. Upon closer examination, however, the signs are there in the people, their clothing, and their art. This enchanting place stands as a monument to times gone by, of progress today and of the future's quest.

Zanzibar—its magic is inviting!

# China, Into the Future!

On a recent trip to China there were many surprises and discoveries. Even though I had seen the modern buildings erected for the 2008 Olympics on TV, I was not prepared for the level of modernization and industrialization evident throughout its cities. And again, even though I knew intellectually that it had the largest population of people in the world; I still was not prepared for the enormity and diversity of their landscape, architecture and lifestyles. Over and over again we were confronted with modern architectural wonders, many side by side with their historical, ancient monuments and structures. No matter how hard I tried, I realized that television and my reading had skewed my impressions of that vast and great nation, one of the oldest civilizations in the world. Even though television has opened up the world for all of us, it can only show part of the truth. Thus, by its nature, doing an injustice to whatever is its focus. To take it all in on the screen is impossible.

Even though modernization has taken hold, the centuries-old structures and major historical and cultural remains are prominently evident. Although changing, with the ways of the western world invading its very foundation, these changes are juxtaposed against the Great Wall of China and so many old world feats of "unbelievability." The 3,000 terracotta soldiers buried beneath what were farms in the Xi'an area are absolutely one of their greatest feats exhibiting the strength, tenacity, artistic skill, cultural traditions, and mighty and powerful controls of the Qin Dynasty as well as those that followed. Even though it was not a part of our trip, we took the opportunity as a side trip to go to Xi'an and to visit the Terracotta soldiers' archaeological wonder. Each of those soldiers, their uniforms, their implements and weapons, the chariots and carriages and the animals were carefully and individually crafted with no two being alike. They were realistic, life-size individuals representing a world unknown today while serving as a reminder of all that was, and preserving the past in its delicate and sometimes ruthless glory! No trip to China is complete without it.

All nations give evidence of their strong and resilient history, their proud traditions and their current progressive movement in this day's world. China is the embodiment of all that is past, present and future. Its future is perhaps brighter and bolder than most. The sheer numbers of people are overwhelming but the talent and traditions of resilience and self-made progress—along with its thirst for what is new and worthy to build the future—appears unequaled in the world.

Of course, Communism still existed but appeared to be changing and even waning in many areas. Those who live in the government-built and owned compartmentalized housing and apartments speak happily of current and planned development to improve and modernize their living conditions. Most of the current apartment buildings are really tall high rises; beyond what we call high-rise in the USA. The individual apartments were generally only five hundred square feet for a family. Most buildings have only two bathrooms on each floor; one for men and one for women. They cook on their woks on the balconies; thus the convenience of everything being in the same pot. Farmers in the rural areas still farm on government-owned plots but capitalism is alive and well, and will eventually invade those inner structures in both the rural and urban areas. Even now, there is plentiful evidence of individual ownership of fabulous dwellings and businesses.

We all hear about and see via television the small narrow streets, the vendors crowding the alleys and streets and the tremendous traffic all about the cities. That is a true depiction of crowding and traffic. However, most surprising was the number of American cars on the streets of Beijing. Although there were other car models, there appeared to be more GM cars in China than in America. Unlike most other places I have visited in European, African and Middle Eastern countries, Mercedes-Benz appeared to be the most prominent "foreign" car.

The realization that China had purchased American cars in what appeared to be huge numbers, provided another perspective on foreign trade and companies building plants and hiring people overseas. It took me back to my childhood when we "traded" toys, baseball cards, comic books, games, and for me it was marbles. Trading meant giving a friend something of yours in exchange for something of theirs; something you both valued but were willing to give up. Similarly, international trade is a two-way street (can and should be); the USA and China are "trading" cars and other goods. Perhaps without the purchase of cars by the Chinese, GM would have folded in America during the economic downturn. If they buy GM cars, then the expectation is that GM will build plants in China and employ

*Slices of Life* | 151

Chinese to operate and work in them. Similarly, if we purchase products from other nations in sufficient bulk, we should expect the same; I think that is happening with Toyota's cars, for example.

However, equally evident and surprising are the evidences of business capitalism and the possibilities of economic and developmental dominance in the world. Its financial structures, though struggling, like those of other nations, hold the promise of emerging as a world financial leader. The people's creativity and innovative feats are readily visible everywhere and rooted in a tradition of artistic and intellectual curiosity and creativity.

It seems that every household, perhaps born of necessity, embodies artistic talents that capture their cultural traditions while displaying their hopes for the future. One feat that appears common in China and perhaps in other cultures as well is that of painting inside bottles. No matter how small the bottle and the opening, they can paint a picture or scene upside down on reverse with small brushes and from the back that emerges as a realistic scene when viewed from the outside of the bottle. I am always amazed at the results and before my visit wondered how it was done. Now knowing, I am even more amazed. It reminds me of woodcut prints that a friend of mine, Roland Watts of Winston Salem, does. Perhaps, this is more a commentary on my lack of artistic talent and knowledge than an amazing feat by artists in China and elsewhere.

We visited several of the country's major cities: Beijing, Shanghai, Xi'an and Hong Kong. Beginning with the modern and abundantly spacious airports, the cities reflect modernity as well as the history of their people and culture. Beijing, China's largest metropolis and the country's capital city has twenty million people with five million in its city center. The other fifteen million are distributed in adjoining metropolitan areas.

Although we all marveled at the Olympic structures and were amazed by their size and architectural creativity, many pre-Olympic buildings are equally innovative and marvelous wonders. Among the most impressive of the structures is the age-old Tiananmen Square. The vastness of the square and the masses of people it holds are remarkable. We all found ourselves admiring the square and all it represented while shuddering at the memories of the youth and other citizens killed there in 1989. The square itself is a wide expanse of both paved and green areas several US city blocks long and wide. Erected just in front of the Imperial Palace or the Forbidden City, an age-old traditional landmark, Tiananmen Square now serves as a symbol of the new China.

One of the traditions observed on the square was that of a small child perhaps two years old dressed for the cool weather who danced and moved to the music being played somewhere on the square. I thought then, this could be anywhere in the world. She became animated as we applauded her every move. Then we realized that there was a slit in her pants between her legs. Someone whispered that it was tradition to leave an opening for children to simply squat and pee or whatever they needed to do whenever. Before long, she did squat and pee but missed only a few beats as she resumed her movement to the music and to our applause.

In a vast Beijing mall akin to our outlet designer stores but larger, we could bargain for pearls, gold, leather, shoes, and products of all sorts but mostly high-end finds. Of course, we had a ball looking for, finding and bargaining for deals. Most bought pearls, bags, and Chinese objects as gifts to take back home. And we felt obligated to leave paper reminders of our visit with the Chinese vendors.

The Chinese have a real handle on controlling emotions or is it feng shui? After having gone through the Imperial Palace and attendant buildings, the dynasty's garden and palace with throngs of people, we emerged and walked through the Sacred Way where the abrupt change in scenery completely changes your mood as if mandating calm and peace. It is in a park-like setting with a very wide stone walkway lined with extra large, twin stone animal statues; lions, camels, elephants, etc. as well as figures of men of power lining each side. The group of giant stone figurines on the ground of the Ming tombs are said to be the best preserved and true-to-life figurines representative of the time. They were obviously skillfully carved. A walk down this way was a solemn, but joyous and uplifting experience. I felt as if I was finding the inner me and peace.

Every culture has its visual and performing arts and seeks to preserve its history through them. The Chinese artistic talents and their resultant products were evident everywhere. In Shanghai, we went to a traditional dance recital. It was a feat to behold and reminded me of the South African troupes that performed their traditional dances. So much of what we see in ballet and modern and popular dance is probably derived from the traditions of this Eastern and African old-world cultures.

Magnificent Hong Kong, the most westernized part of China and once an English colony remains more capitalistic and western-like than the other Chinese cities. There were bargains galore and many of our group had custom clothing of the finest materials, especially silk, and craftsmanship made and delivered a day later at a significantly lower price than could be obtained in the US. Shopping there was a supreme treat! Not only could you get designer everything at a steal, there was Chinese Obama paraphernalia everywhere with captions in both Chinese and English. Of course I bought up as much as I could and brought it back home.

Hong Kong was also where we watched the presidential election of 2008 unfold. We set ourselves up with a reserved conference room in the Shangri La Hotel and *hors d'oeuvres* ready for a party as we watched the returns on CNN. Many Chinese and other hotel guests came by and it seemed that all of Hong Kong was celebrating the election of Obama.

Hong Kong is one of the most beautiful cities anywhere. Feng shui must have derived from the natural surroundings in all of China and especially Hong Kong. As I stood at the top of Victoria Peak in Stanley Park it seemed that mountains, rivers, forested areas, and beautiful land are Hong Kong's and China's trademark. The environment seems to be balanced and generally the Chinese take advantage of their natural resources in framing the cities, countryside and living. From Victoria Peak, it seems one can see forever. Artists paint the popular scenes of the harbor below, dotted with the Chinese dhows, tourist ferries and mega yachts. What a beautiful sight! I could not help but purchase several paintings and even have the artists to paint the scenes I chose.

Before leaving Victoria Peak we were compelled again to share our American resources with the shopkeepers at the upscale Peak Galleria and Piazza where the sights and shopping were divine. Later in the evening, a hometown friend's son (the Brickler's) who lived and worked in Hong Kong took me and some of my friends to dinner at the Café Deco. We had dinner on the balcony and enjoyed the spectacular views of Hong Kong Island, Victoria and Kowloon. What a wonderful way to end one of my favorite trips of a lifetime!

# Jamaica, No Problem Mon at Dunn's River Falls

**Dunn's River Falls**, a Jamaican jewel, presents a challenge for the courageous, a treat to be enjoyed, and an ultimate thrill that gets the adrenaline flowing wildly. It will leave you breathless with the sight of its beauty, the thrill of its challenge, and the comfort of its soothing waters.

As the water rushes toward me, and then nearly sweeps me away, I am comforted little by the human chain, holding hands to climb the slippery rocks six hundred feet up. Of course, I can't see the entire curvy, sloping climb as the water cascades down the massive, cragged rocks. If I could, I might not have attempted it. But I thought it would be fun. I occasionally slip and break the chain linked by hands clasped by my son in front of me, and my nephew behind me. Presumably, I'm safely cradled between the two hunks. After the initial entry, the water becomes increasingly comfortable and comforting. Reaching one level that looked like the end, we paused for a natural Jacuzzi treatment. It felt like a soothing spa with water rushing down my back, and as I attempted to turn around to equalize the treatment in front, I was swept by the waves rushing from above. So, I had a dunking with no help from anyone except the force of the water. I thought we were near the end, but as the river bent and curved there was more to climb. I am wet from head to toe, and throughout as well. I can hardly enjoy the tremendous scenery of water, rocks, and foliage for watching my steps to keep my footing, and to be sure to follow my son's footsteps.

*Swoosh, swoosh!* The water races down the slopes with a force great enough to carry me away. I hold on tightly to my companions while occasionally slipping, and extricating my hand from one of the guys to hold on to a rock, but the water won't let me hold on for long. It is thrilling and scary and if I have ever been wide-eyed—this was it. Luckily, I had my glasses on to partially shield my eyes from the water. No one told me I needed goggles. And of course, I who hadn't recently been challenged like this didn't think of them or even water shoes. What was I thinking? After observing that just about everyone else had water shoes, I bought some on the way to the falls.

When we finally reached the top, I kept looking around the bend for more, because we had reached what I thought was the top before, and each time there was more to come. The human chain of about twenty-five people climbing the rocks in forceful, rushing waters seemed endless. We passed word along the chain about potential threats and challenges; "the rocks ahead are extra slippery; watch your step; the next step is very steep; the water is especially strong here so hold onto your partners." It was team work at its best with a skilled pair of leaders, photographers, and videographers to make sure that we never lost the moments. Our group was old like me, and even older, young, and the very young like an eight-year-old, and all ages in between. We were black, white, Hispanic, Caribbean, European, African, Asian, and blends of all sorts! Wouldn't it be lovely if this teamwork and diversity could be manifested in all that we do?

One last *swoosh* and I was out of the water for the day with red eyes, a salty taste in my mouth, wet hair, clothes and body, and a new set of partners. What an absolutely thrilling experience! One of the world's natural spas, beauty spots, and challenges, Dunn's River Falls is a Jamaican jewel; one that you shouldn't miss in your travel to the Ocho Rios, Jamaica area.

# Aging

# Living Elegantly, Aging Gracefully

(LEAG)

As I approached sixty, age became a minor but fleeting consideration. But as I entered the seventies it became a bit more of a concern. I didn't think of myself as "old" nor did I think I looked old. I had had a few surgeries by then, but I had a few even during childhood and on up through early adulthood. So that was certainly not a marker or a symbol of getting old. I even said to myself as a few gray hairs snuck in and were persistent in staying power that I liked gray hair and it is not a symptom of getting old. I suppose that I was in a state of denial. Now, I have never looked upon aging as a bad thing. I really do like the gray hair and the wisdom that seems to be the halo of age.

However, there are some symptoms of aging that I resent and fear. When I started seeing the dimples in my thighs, the proper term is *cellulite*, the expanded waistline, the fat in the belly, and especially the slight sagging in the facial skin, and, of course, the sagging breast, I really got busy walking and later even going to the gym. Last year, I started working out with a trainer. When I slack up on the exercise, it's mostly because of travel or involvement in some other community activity, however, the sags and wrinkles (S and W) come creeping back. Dare I look in the mirror and see the S-and-W condition emerging. That is enough reason to cancel everything and head on out to Lake Ella, my favorite walking spot, and do a minimum of five rounds or three miles. If I continue on a steady regimen for a few weeks, I walk as many as ten rounds or six miles. But these days that seldom happens. Plus, getting into a regimen of cleansing and moisturizing the face and neck is a must to hold the crow's feet, wrinkles, and sagging skin at bay (CFW and SS). You might delay or minimize them, but they have more staying power than you do. They will win in the end. So it appears that fighting the bulge and CFW and SS is going to be a permanent pursuit.

You can run, but you can't hide. Age will catch you if you continue to live. The only way to avoid getting old is to die. Well, I don't like that option, and when it catches you, make sure you are in the best shape that you can be so that you can ward off some of the more devastating effects like wrinkles, sagging, fat and more fat, heart attacks, strokes diabetes, arthritis, etc.

Of course, being in shape has a far-reaching impact. You are more flexible, balanced, and feel more relaxed and able to go and do more. You can rest better, and if you continue on a regular regimen, exercise becomes a necessity, an attractive activity. It's like an addiction. You have to do it. Thus, staying in shape rewards you with an active lifestyle and allows you to enjoy the better and even the mundane things of life. As we all know, we also have to couple that with eating the right foods. That combination of exercise and eating right makes a big difference in our ability to control our weight, and perhaps prevent or control major bad health conditions like diabetes, strokes, heart attacks, and others. I haven't mastered the latter yet, eating that is.

I'll eat right for a couple of days or even a week or two, but then the intent just gives way to overwhelming desire. I go into sugar withdrawal and give in. I understand the plight of the drug addict. Even though my addiction is not drugs, the body's reaction is probably the same.

I can even control my lifelong habit of taking my drug of choice, sweets, if I can have fruit as a substitute. So I eat the fruit not just an apple or small portions of melon; I really eat them. I can kill off a half melon each day—a big one. I also have an affinity for nuts peanuts, pecans, walnuts, and just about any others. As I sat eating a bag of raw peanuts one day, my mom said to me, "You claim you're on a diet but you eat peanuts like they will soon be off the market. Don't you know that they feed peanuts to hogs to fatten them up?" She always had a way of bringing you down to earth as you floated in the cloud of disbelief.

So when I say to my doctor that I don't know why I am not losing weight because I eat only veggies, fruits, nuts, lean meats like mostly seafood and only an occasional beef or pork meal and I seldom eat fried foods. Finally, the doctor asks, "How much of each do you eat and which fruits?" "Oh well," I say, "I really eat a lot of fruit." The doc responds, "There is sugar in fruit and sugar is sugar. You can eat some fruit but not to the extent that you are doing. Try and limit the amount of fruit and eat the types that have less sugar and are more filling." He also cautioned me that even though nuts are healthy foods, they are stacked with fat. So I was cautioned to eat nuts sparingly. In my head, I am thinking, "You 'gotta be out of your mind!'" . . . But in the end I know that he is right and I half-heartedly vow to try. It just never seems to work out for long.

The physical shape we're in helps to mold our mental, emotional, and social condition and our outlook and perspective on life. If we could only look ahead and see what the future holds while we are young, we would choose to live our lives differently. Although we will always encounter differences in all kind of ways, we are most likely to fear those with differences of opinions, attitudes, and other personality traits that we may consider negative in comparison to our own. Often these differences result in getting "mad" at the other person simply because she disagrees.

As you age and if you become wiser, you realize that it doesn't matter and if the other person makes you uncomfortable, just walk away when you don't have to be in her company. The most important thing is to not get angry or at least not to carry that excess baggage around. If you carry the burden of anger and even hate; it eats at your core; you are distressed, and in severe cases, it could actually make you ill. Who knows, the other person may not even feel that way and is going about her business and enjoying life while you are stuck with your anger and hatred, eating at your stomach, intestines, colon, heart, etc., and thus your proper functioning.

Why not just avoid the company of any person who makes you uncomfortable. Surround yourself with friends and those whose company you enjoy. No one wants to be loaded down with your problems all the time. It is necessary to share your woes occasionally with those closest to you but to dwell on them and make the relationship only about your problems will sour any relationship. The person you're taking your problems to has problems of her own, so dealing with yours and hers is a double weight on her. Get a psychologist or psychiatrist if you need that kind of therapy.

Find things that you enjoy doing and do them! If your passion is gardening, then go at it with all abandon. If you like to draw or write then get busy doing it. For most of us, there is no one thing but perhaps several. I enjoy reading, writing, and walking in a natural habitat with water, plants, trees, birds, fish, and other marine animals, the change of scenery in spring and the lush palette of fall, the icicles hanging on trees in winter and snow-laden scenes of the country side, boat rides in the summer, traveling and the companionship of special people. I also enjoy just being in the company of other friends and family, informally chatting, laughing, reliving our stories, and watching the future happen through our children. Helping others and giving of ourselves to those in need provides a level of satisfaction unlike any other. You will know that you have done something to advance the world even though it may be just one person. We will find that pursuing our passions rewards us with enormous joy.

The most important discovery that we can make in our lives is our true selves. Who are you? Who am I? We'll then know what to hang on our walls, what keepsakes to keep and why, which books to leave on our shelves, and which can be discarded. Equally important is our outlook on life—is it positive or negative or somewhere in between. If it is anything but positive, work to increase the positives. The negative outlook will only wear you down. We've all encountered people who criticize everything and everybody. They can't seem to see the beauty, the fullness that is life, and only look at the underside—the negative. If someone says, "That is a beautiful arrangement!" They will say, "It should have had more roses, and the baby's breath is not right!" You know them and if you can't help them to be more positive, avoid them or limit your contact with them. They will bring you down and have you feeling sad and negative. Seek out the company of people who have a bright outlook on life and provide joy, laughter, and comfort. Seek out beauty in people as you would beauty in objects.

The older I get, the more I rewind the tapes. I see myself becoming my mother, and I realize that in all of life through the hustle, bustle of work, raising a family, doing what it is we have to do, keeping up with the Joneses for some, and all the myriad of other things we feel we have to do, matter little in the big scheme that is life. We don't need the commercial fashions, electronics, cars, homes, and toys we surround ourselves with. We can be happy with those things we love and cherish. They can be expensive, but they can also be and are more likely to be simple and inexpensive. What about a photo of your parents; you and the family on an outing; that little painted rock; or the roughly shaped clay pig that your son gave you when he was in first grade; the soup tureen that your niece made for you; the framed dried flower from another niece? The tiny ceramic duck your nephews gave you when they were young? Most are likely to be inexpensive but are worth millions to you. You get the picture. Display them attractively and enjoy them every day. They will elegantly frame your picture show and bring you joy.

What matters most is that we live our lives so that we create as many good memories as possible. Of course, we couldn't escape some catastrophes. After all, these are what help us to be strong and to experience and appreciate joy. Live while you are living, for death will come whether we are prepared or not. Like the old saying goes, there is no sunshine without rain. As I visit hospitals, nursing homes, and the elderly in their homes, I wonder what's playing on their radio or TV or video; the one in their heads. I asked my mom near the end of her life if she had some good memories and to share them with me. Wow! What a storehouse of excitement, commitment, love, and absolute unselfishness that came through those moments. The movie playing in her head was indeed an academy award winner with exceptional joy sprinkled with sadness, regrets, and sorrow.

I hope that my movie is in 3-D or whatever is the best medium of the time, filled with love, that special someone, the people I enjoy, the scenes of happiness as well as those that will at times make me sad. And I hope that my scenery reflects the things I hold dear—my books, my art, select whatnots, not because they are expensive, but because they were given to me by special people and thus have special meaning; my home's décor featuring my art and glass collections, the lushness of God's landscape of beautiful flowers, plants, trees and waterways, and mountains I have enjoyed. That is the essence of living elegantly while aging gracefully.

Edwards Brothers, Inc.
Thorofare, NJ USA
March 12, 2012